Pilgrimage of a Country Preacher...

...A Journey to the Holy Land of Appalachia

by
Father Ralph W. Beiting
with Tom Pelletier

Front cover photo by Margaret Gabriel
Back cover photo by Ken Craven

Father Beiting's previous books on the Christian
Appalachian Project and his life include:

God Can Move Mountains
Appalachia . . . a Special Place . . . A Bridge of Hope
Promises To Keep . . . A Vision for Appalachia
Dreams of Faith
Called to the Mountains . . . The Autobiography of
Reverend Ralph W. Beiting
Frontier of the Heart . . . The Search for
Heroes in Appalachia

Copies of these books can be
obtained by writing to:
Christian Appalachian Project
322 Crab Orchard Road
Lancaster, KY 40446-0001

TABLE OF CONTENTS

Dedication

These reflections are dedicated
to my family,
my fellow priests and other religious friends,
and to the countless host of parishioners,
volunteers, CAP workers, and supporters
who have made this pilgrimage
possible and inspiring.

May all of you continue to
take the road less traveled.

Christian Appalachian Project
1964-1995

More than forty five years ago, Father Ralph W. Beiting was called to Appalachia to build church communities and ease the pain caused by poverty. In 1957, he founded an interdenominational Christian organization called Cliffview Lodge that in 1964 became the Christian Appalachian Project (CAP). By offering long-term, self-help solutions to the problems that hold Appalachia's people back, CAP gives the poor a chance to work themselves out of poverty and to see themselves as they truly are, the people of God.

CAP provides educational programs for children and adults, home repair assistance, business-development programs, elderly visitation programs, emergency relief assistance, and so many other efforts. With over seventy programs and activities, CAP brings hope and peace to those in need.

Through the generous work of thousands of volunteers, hundreds of local workers, and a host of loyal supporters from all over the country, CAP has become one of the largest relief organizations in America, and a pioneer in the development of programs to defeat poverty and inspire hope.

Prologue –
The Holy Land of
Appalachia

For two thousand years, Christians have been making pilgrimages to the Holy Land in Palestine to be close to the source of their faith — to be close to Jesus. Even today, pilgrims hope that by walking where Jesus walked they can know Him and understand His love for the world.

I have come to believe that there is an even better way to know Jesus, and that is to walk, not where He walked 2,000 years ago, but where He walks today. To follow Him throughout your life is the greatest pilgrimage of all.

I have also come to learn, at the tender age of 71, that to find Jesus and follow Him you have to go where His people are. You have to go where people need Him most because that is where His presence is most easily felt.

The poverty-stricken areas of Appalachia are such places.

It is here that Jesus' footsteps echo softly as He visits His people in the mountains.

One of my favorite places to think and pray is on
my back porch in Louisa, Kentucky. On that porch
at the end of a long day some months ago, I began
thinking about pilgrimages. The Big Sandy River is
just a stone's throw from my porch and, especially
at night, the gentle noise of the river instills quiet
and peace in my soul. The past seemed close at hand
that night.

The more I thought, the more I came to see my
whole life as a pilgrimage — looking for Jesus' footsteps in Appalachia. I also felt it was time for me to
go back to the beginning and be refreshed and re-
newed before I started out again on the long road
that lay ahead.

"I need to retrace the roads I have traveled the last
45 years," I said to the Big Sandy River. "I need to
see the creeks and hollers and look out over the mountains that were my first home. I want to find the folks
I once knew, and remember those who have passed
away. I need to touch the earth again and feel the
waters of the land that has been home to me."

As anyone who knows me would attest, once I get
an idea in my head I don't easily let go, so off I
started — on a pilgrimage of my own. More than a
thousand years ago, a pilgrim headed for the Holy
Land might have made the journey on the back of a
donkey, but this being a modern age, I set out by
automobile. I drove over many of the miles I have
traveled, and relived the memories of nearly a half a
century of living in Appalachia. Seeing so many of

the places where the Church and the Christian Appalachian Project have changed the lives of people trapped in poverty made me realize just how much has happened on my journey.

How could so much have come from that simple beginning in 1950? I consider myself a fairly intelligent person, clever with my hands, and good with people. I know I have a lot of energy and that when I talk, people tend to listen.

But still, far too much has happened for this to be my doing. I would have had to be a superman to do all this myself. I would have had to be God.

Of course, it wasn't me who did all this. It was God. He and the wonderful people, His believers, who joined me when their pilgrimages crossed the path of mine. I am only one pilgrim following the trail of Jesus, but over the years I've been joined by thousands of volunteers, dedicated employees, other priests and ministers, and generous supporters from around the country.

As I journeyed last fall, retracing the years of my pilgrimage, memories and dreams came back to me. I was struck by how small those dreams were in the early years. They were tiny, limited to a small space and to small resources. When I started, I had less than $100 to my name. I was the only Catholic priest in a four county area — an area the size of the state of Rhode Island. Fewer than one out of a thousand people in these counties were Catholic. I didn't know a soul there, Catholic or not. I was a stranger with no connection or home.

I should have been too frightened by loneliness
and isolation to dream at all. Yet I was convinced
that I was never alone and that the greatest dreamer
of all was always by my side.

My first home was a run-down house on Chestnut
Street in Berea, Kentucky. Before I even moved in
my small bundle of belongings, I hung a crucifix on
the wall of what would be my bedroom. I know that
many non-Catholic Christians — some of my best
friends — don't use the crucifix as a symbol of
Christ's presence. But to me, it has always held deep
meaning. I needed to see Him and realize how deeply
He could love.

I ached with terrible loneliness and doubt each
morning when I woke up and each evening when I
went to bed, but when I looked at that cross, I knew
I could never, ever find a genuine reason for quitting.

Jesus didn't. With Him as my model and my
strength, I knew this pilgrimage must begin and pros-
per.

And I was right. What started as one man walking
down a dark road has become a mighty throng of
good people of every faith and creed, walking hand
in hand towards the beautiful goal of restoring hope
and promise in Appalachia.

In medieval times, when a pilgrim returned from
the Holy Land, he or she would be considered a hero
and people would gather to hear fantastic tales of the

arduous and dangerous journey. Hopefully, my pilgrimage is not yet ending, but I know it can't go on forever. It is after all, 1995. I am more than 71 years old, and I have been a pilgrim for 45 years. This seems like a good time to sit down for a little while and look back on the journey.

I'm not asking for any kind of hero's welcome, but I hope you will humor me and let me share a few memories and thoughts. I hope you will find them interesting. I hope, even more, that you will find in them the inspiration to continue your own pilgrimage toward our Lord.

Join me as I walk through 45 years of pilgrimage and come join with me on a new pilgrimage into the future. I have walked a long way in 45 years, but I am convinced that the real journey is only just beginning. The best is yet to be. Come with me on a pilgrimage to find Jesus and walk where He walked.

While Appalachia has no sacred shrines, no running waters where Jesus stood, no open tombs where the dead once rested, it is still to me a Holy Land, a place touched by God with beauty and grace. It is a place where Jesus needs to be seen. A place to be enlightened by faith.

Come with me to the Holy Land of Appalachia.

God Leads the Way

The first steps of a pilgrimage are always taken with a mixture of sadness, excitement . . . and sheer terror. When I began to retrace my steps, I went back to that first day, October 7, 1950, the day I arrived in Berea, Kentucky. I parked my car in front of the house where I lived in Berea 45 years earlier, and all the emotions of that first day came rushing back to me.

I was terribly sad that day in 1950 because I was leaving so much behind. I was moving farther from my parents' home, a wonderful place, full of life and the love of my parents and my ten brothers and sisters. We all cried the day I left.

I was also leaving my first parish, St. Bernard in Dayton, Kentucky, where I had made many loving and caring friends.

But I remember that the day I left was also one of great excitement. I had been assigned to four counties in southeastern Kentucky: Madison, Jackson, Rockcastle, and Garrard. My first objective was to create a chapel in Berea.

I was 26 years old, only a year out of seminary, and I was thrilled to have such a big responsibility so soon.

Before that day was out, however, I was to know the terror that responsibility can bring.

The bishop had bought a small house in Berea that was meant to be my home and chapel. When I first drove up to it in 1950, it hardly looked fit for either.

I parked in a gravel driveway with deep potholes. As I peered across five foot high weeds, I could see a sad old house.

The porch had rotted and was dotted with holes. Every step on its decaying planks threatened to create a new hole. Once I made it safely past that danger and into the house, I found that the entire bottom floor had sagged. The previous owners had dug a room under the house for a coal-fired furnace. They miscalculated the size of the furnace, however, and when the time came to install it, they made extra room by cutting the beam that supported the floor joists. That had been many years before. The coal furnace was already old and weak. Without adequate support, the floor had sagged.

I walked around the house gingerly, not wanting to add to the sag of the floor, and I felt the weight of the challenge in front of me. I imagine the pilgrims of old probably felt the same way after their first day on the long, long trail to the Holy Land. "What have I gotten myself into?" I asked.

I thought about my meager resources. I had less than $100 in my pocket. My monthly salary as a priest was $41. There were only nine Catholics in the area — three of them children — so I couldn't rely on much financial support from them.

I had learned, growing up during the Great Depression, that if you never give up you can't fail. But that lesson had been proven in the company of supportive relatives and neighbors. My religious training said that with God you can do all things. But those comfortable words had been taught to me in a warm home and in comfortable classrooms surrounded by friends and teachers.

Were these ideas real in this faraway place?

On my first night in Berea there were no relatives to lean on. I hadn't met my neighbors yet, never mind developed the friendships that would allow me to count on them. There was little comfort. In fact, that old coal furnace was so bad that the house was barely warmer than the chilly October air outside.

Worst of all was the quiet. It was awful. I had grown up in a home with 13 people, where the sound of human voices was constant. There in that abandoned old house in Berea, quiet permeated the walls and floors. The awful stillness only emphasized the loneliness.

For a few moments, I panicked. Should I turn back from this foolish pilgrimage? Should I get into my car and go back up north? In just a few hours I could be back home with my family.

I thought, "I am only 26 years old. I was ordained only a year ago. I have so much to learn. Shouldn't a more experienced man take up this enormous challenge?"

I went upstairs to where my bedroom would be. I looked at the bare room, with just a bed and a chair. I hung the crucifix that had been given to me as a religion award in high school. I sat on the chair and looked at the man on the crucifix. Things hadn't gone well for Him either. Until that moment, that crucifix had been primarily a reminder to me of my high school accomplishment. Now, slowly I began to see the man on the cross and forget the engraving with my name.

I began to talk to God and His Son. "Please don't leave me alone here," I said. "I don't know where I'm going. I don't know how to get there. Will you let me hold your hand and let me walk at your side? Will you talk to me? Will you comfort me? Will you forgive me when I fail?"

There was no miraculous answer. I didn't see the cross move, or Jesus smile at me. But God's words from the Bible came to my mind. "Come follow me. I will never leave you an orphan. Fear not you of little faith. Did you not know I was with you? With me you can do all things. It is only when you are without me that you can do nothing." I remembered Peter's words to the early persecuted Christians in Asia Minor, "Cast all your cares on Him, for He loves you." I remembered Saint Paul's reminder to the citizens of Rome, "I can do all things in Him who strengthens me."

Finally, I got up and walked downstairs. As I walked through the rooms of the house, my imagination began to work. That room would make a good sanctuary. I could put the altar there, the pulpit there, and the tabernacle over here. If I took out walls, I could put pews or chairs in these two rooms over here for the people I hoped would come to this little church. The sanctuary could go over here, and this could be an office. I could redo this kitchen and dining area.

Strengthened by those dreams, I went outside. There was a full moon and the mountains were outlined against a sky with too many stars to count. A few cars moved slowly down the street. Here and there a person walked toward home.

Suddenly I got the feeling of being very small in God's amazing world. "This is His place," I thought. "It isn't mine or anyone else's. This is God's land, His sky, His people."

For the first time, I ceased thinking of myself as the center of the universe. God was. He had the interest, the care, the longing. I was entering into His world, assisting in His work. He wanted a solution, a new beginning, more than I ever could. All I needed to do was follow the path He was trodding. I thanked Him that night because I had found a Father, a Guide, a Protector, a real Friend, as well as a Redeemer. I didn't know where we were going or how we were going to get there, but I knew that all I had to do was hold His hand and keep walking.

In the 45 years since that night, I have never doubted or changed my mind. He is and has been my wisdom and power. I look at some new problem or opportunity and ask, "What would He do? What is He telling me?"

If I'm sure I have His answer, then I do it. It doesn't matter if it seems reasonable or not. It doesn't matter if I have the money or not. I try to do it.

For example, I promised God that night that I would build Him as many homes as I could. It was a ridiculous promise. I didn't have any land. I didn't have any money or any plans. Yet, in 45 years I have built nine churches in eight different counties. I have helped obtain the land and contributed to the cost and construction of four more. I'm presently helping in the construction of three more. Soon it will be sixteen churches overall.

But more important than me keeping my word to God has been the way God has kept His promises to me. I always asked myself three questions. First, what is the real and persistent need? Second, what is the best solution to that need? And third, are you going to do this for yourself or for God? If I could honestly tell myself it was for God, then I went forward.

Never has He let me down.

For example, I will tell later, when I get to the Lancaster, Kentucky, part of my pilgrimage, about a camp for children that we created. I felt very strongly that God wanted this camp built to bring joy into the lives of His little ones who lived in poverty. But I

didn't have any idea how or where to build a camp.
"Where do I start, Lord?" I prayed. "Where do I go?"

The day I said that prayer, a man knocked on my
door. It was Cliff Ledford, a local realtor.

"I heard you were interested in buying land for a
camp," Cliff said. "Well, I'm trying to sell some lots
on a lake nearby. I wonder if you would be interested?"

I couldn't believe my ears. "Take me to the lake,"
I said.

The lake was lovely. I knew right away that it was
where God wanted that camp to be.

"How much?" I asked.

"Only $1,000 per lot," he said.

"Would you take $500?"

"If you buy all eleven," he said, "I'll take $5,000."

We shook hands and put the paperwork in
motion — even though I hadn't the foggiest idea
where I'd find the money. $5,000 was a lot of money
in those days. It still is today.

A few days later, I received an anonymous gift of
$5,000.

That night I thought back to my prayer and the
knock on my door. Even though that visitor looked
like Cliff Ledford, I knew it was God.

Another time, I had been thinking and praying
about expanding our programs in Jackson County. A
man came to my door and said he had heard that I
was looking for land. He said he was moving and
needed to sell his land quickly. The property was 80

acres with a small house and a barn. It seemed too good to be true. The man said he would sell the entire property for $4,500 if I could come up with the money in six weeks.

That night I prayed to the Lord again. "Where am I going to get $4,500?" I asked Him, but there was no answer. Or so I thought.

The next day, a priest friend of mine called and asked if I'd come up to his parish, Christ the King parish in Lexington, Kentucky (now the cathedral parish of the new Lexington Diocese), the following week and talk to the men of the parish about what I was doing in the mountains. I did, and I told the men about the churches I was building and what I was doing to help the poor.

In the question and answer period, one man asked, "Do you have a special project that you need help with?"

I told them about the 80 acres and my dream to use this as a base for the work I wanted to do in Jackson County. The men listened politely. They gave me a sandwich, a slice of cake, a soft drink, and a check for $100.

I was very grateful and thought the matter was closed. A week later I got a call from one of the men who had been at the meeting. He told me that seven of the men had gotten together, gone to their bank in Lexington and borrowed $4,500 to purchase the land. With unbelievable gratitude, I thanked him.

That night, I looked at the crucifix on my wall in

that little house in Berea and I said to God, "You sure do get around don't you?"

All these memories came back as I stood reminiscing next to that little house in Berea. I remembered another time when God interceded on my behalf.

I hadn't been in Berea a week when a petition began circulating to have me and the Catholic Church thrown out of the town. Just what I needed to ease my sense of isolation.

I found out that my next door neighbor had started the petition. He distrusted Catholics and didn't want to see me get established in his town, never mind right next door.

I tried to talk to him to see if we could find some common ground, but he was adamant that the Catholic Church wasn't needed in his community and that, as a Catholic priest, I could never be his friend.

His petition failed to get me out of town, but he let me know his feelings hadn't changed.

Over time, he became more civil. Still, when he sold us his house for use as a rectory for the church and a place for our volunteers to live, I figured it was so he could get away from us.

I didn't realize how much his perspective had changed until about twenty years later. I was meeting in Berea with various community leaders about a new project, and several people voiced objections. Then my ex-neighbor stood up.

I thought, "Oh no. This is it."

He cleared his throat and looked a little uncomfortable. Then he said, "Well, I've come to believe that Father is the only minister in town who's worth a damn."

I almost fell off my chair. I was especially shocked that he called me "Father," because that title is such a symbol of Catholicism that I didn't think he would ever let it pass his lips in reference to me.

My neighbor went on to say, "You all know I was against Father when he came here, but he's done so much good and has gotten so many other people thinking about how they can help others, I just want him to know that I appreciate him."

I don't think I'll ever get an award or accolade as fulfilling or as unexpected as that one. And I truly believe God must have played a role in my neighbor's change of heart about me.

If I had known all the ways that God would watch over me through the years, I would have celebrated my great fortune. But I couldn't possibly have known all that when I stood there on the overgrown lawn of that poor run-down house on my first night in Appalachia. All I knew was that I had to trust.

So that's what I did. Eventually, that little house became quite beautiful. We repaired and remodeled it and it became quite literally a house of God, filled with joy, celebration, and worship. It was my home and I will always remember it fondly.

But even more, I will always remember the way God took me by the hand and said, "Don't worry, you timid pilgrim. Just walk with Me."

Over the years, He has been my treasure, my pearl of great price. He constantly lets me know that He loves me and He loves this land and the people who make it home. I found in Him the greatest treasure of my life, a Father who cares for me and for us all. I thank Him every day for allowing me to walk with Him and to dream with Him and to start new things for Him.

He has been a God to me, all powerful and all wise. But, He has also been my best friend, my constant companion on this pilgrimage of my life.

Helping Weary Pilgrims Along the Road

There's nothing like meeting someone whose troubles are worse than your own for curing a pilgrim of weariness. That's what happened to me shortly after I moved to Berea.

Because that little house was on the main street, people often stopped to talk when I was cleaning and painting. A mile or so down that road was an area where several poor black families lived. They often stopped to talk and when we became friends, they invited me to their homes. The experience was quite a shock. My sad old house in Berea was a sparkling mansion compared to some of the places where these families lived. Many of the homes had plastic for windows. Many didn't have electricity and were lit by candles at night. Few had running water or an indoor bathroom.

I'll never forget the home of one family. I brought them some food and clothes, and when I went into the house to put the things down, I couldn't help but

notice that one room was missing many of its floor-
boards.

"What happened in there?" I asked.

The father of the family told me, "Well, it's been
awfully cold, and we didn't have no money for wood
or coal, so we pulled up some of them boards and
used 'em for firewood."

Meeting with those families, I got my first glimpses
of the terrible poverty that existed off the main roads
of Appalachia, and realized that the journey I was on
would be a long one.

In those early days in Berea, I would make the long
drive to where my parents lived to collect food, clothing, furniture and other essentials. Then I'd drive back
to Berea and deliver these gifts to families in great
need.

The more people I helped, the more I noticed the
enormous needs. Families were without adequate
food. Without electricity. Without proper clothing.

I knew that I had to share with these fellow pilgrims. There had to be a way for me to offer assistance along the road.

It was obvious that my trips back and forth with
food and clothing were not enough. I expanded that
effort and we created rummage stores. Later, these
early efforts would develop into CAP's Attic Stores
and its Emergency Assistance program.

I knew that people needed to have food, clothing,
and furniture, but I also knew that they needed far
more than just those material things.

I wanted our rummage stores to provide something even more important — hope. I have always wanted our stores to be places of companionship. I wanted the people who staffed the stores to be more than just shopkeepers. I wanted them to be friends to the people we served.

Barbara was one such friend. She was always anxious to get to work at the Attic Store because she considered the people who came into the Store her neighbors. Many of her "customers" came in just to talk. Sometimes they came to tell her about a problem. Most often, they came to see if she would pray for them.

I suspect that Barbara did more praying in public than any of us ministers. She was always there for anyone who needed her. As one of her customers left with clothing or a pair of shoes or a can of beans, they also took something else with them. They took home the feeling that God cared and that they were not forgotten on their journey. Barbara had that kind of effect on people.

I think God blessed our efforts as much for the companionship we were providing to His isolated mountain folk as for the food and clothing. He was the one who said, after all, that, "Man does not live on bread alone."

For example, after we had created a rummage store in Berea, we wanted to have one in Mt. Vernon, in Rockcastle County. We rented an old grocery store. It was ramshackled and needed a lot of work, but it was right on the main street.

We fixed the place up as much as we could and opened it a few months later. My father and mother were living nearby because my father was helping me build a church in Mt. Vernon, Kentucky. My mother and another lady, Mrs. O'Neal, who came all the way from Maine to volunteer, ran the rummage store. They turned it into a gem. It became a community center where whole families would come for companionship. We had story hours for kids, evening classes for adults, and more.

It eventually became our most successful rummage store, but we nearly lost it.

Unfortunately, the owner of the old store that was our Attic died and the building was put up for public auction. Even though we were doing a great deal of good, I knew there were people in the community who didn't want us there and who would outbid me just to get rid of us.

I talked to Travis, a man who lived in Lancaster, Kentucky, who was unknown in Mt. Vernon. I said, "Travis, I want you to go to the auction and bid on this building. But don't start until I quit. If I don't start first, they'll know something is funny. When I stop bidding, you go on in $500 increments and let's see how things come out."

There was a big crowd at the auction but Travis and I were the only ones who knew the plan. Even the other CAP volunteers expected me to do all the bidding for CAP. The bidding started and quickly got to $30,000. Then $30,500. At that point, I stopped.

The auctioneer came to me and said, "Father Beiting, you can't stop. You are doing so much with that building."

"No," I said. "It's too much. We'll have to let it go."

Travis bid $31,000. Someone else bid $31,500. Travis wanted to look at me for approval but I had told him not to. He bid $32,000.

"Going once. Going twice. Gone. Sold for $32,000."

When it was over, the auctioneer went to Travis and asked him how he wanted the deed made out. Travis turned to me and said, "I don't know, you'll have to ask Father Beiting."

There was a rush of confused, angry voices, but in the end, the bid held and we got the store for $32,000. I later found out that the group that wanted us out of town had made arrangements for a line of credit for $50,000. They didn't want the property, they just wanted to stop what we were doing. I'll never understand why. In the end, I think God stepped in with us and made sure we could continue to provide for the physical and spiritual needs of His people.

In addition to the Attics, we set up emergency assistance offices throughout our counties where weary pilgrims can receive a helping hand. We provide a great deal of material and monetary assistance to people facing a crisis.

Too many people in Appalachia live in homes not

much better than the ones I visited in Berea so many
years ago. Many homes are heated by coal or wood,
or have old, cracked wiring. That's why we have an
unusually high number of fires here. Unfortunately,
homes often burn to the ground because they are so
isolated and it's hard for the fire trucks to reach them
in time.

When families get burned out, we provide food,
clothing, furniture, and aid in finding a new home.

We also have many medical needs here. The scar-
city of medical resources and the poverty of many
families often creates crises. Not long ago, a mother
came to ask for my help because her little daughter
was going blind. The girl needed an operation but
the nearest place to have it done was Columbus, Ohio,
200 miles away.

The woman had applied for all the kinds of assistance she could and she was still short the $500 they
needed to make the trip.

Needless to say, I found a way to help her.

These are the problems some of our fellow pilgrims
face. We do everything we can to help, but the aid
we give is more than just monetary. We also offer
friendship. We welcome people in need into the large
and still growing CAP family.

"Please join us," we say. "There's plenty of room
in this family for all."

When we do this, we find we aren't just gaining a
new family member to support, we are gaining a new
family member with special gifts for all. So many of

the people who once came to us for emergency help offer their help in return.

It's their way of saying, "Thanks for helping me out when I was down. Now that I have a little strength myself, I'll lend a hand to another weary traveler."

There are many ways that our fellow pilgrims need help on this long road of life. I often visit people in prison. I always find this very sad. Not only for the young men, for most of the prisoners are young men, but also for their families. Every time I visit at a prison, the waiting room is full of young women with babies. I always wonder what their lives will be like. What will the child's life be like growing up in such sad circumstances?

It makes me curse the poverty and lack of hope that drives young men to crime.

Other pilgrims who need our friendship are the sick. An old friend is now in a nursing home. She shares her room with another woman who is feeble and losing her hearing. At the end of my visits with my friend I always give her a blessing. The other woman always cries out, "Pray for me too, Father, before you go. Pray for me! Give me one of those blessings." When I go over to her bed to bless her, she grabs my hands and says, "You'll always pray for me, won't you?"

I think of all the places where CAP shares with pilgrims in need. I have always thought that to offer help to another human being in need is one of the most rewarding things a person can do.

I thank God for the weary travelers He has brought to my side. There is hardly a road in this area that doesn't hold a memory of someone who cried out for help. There is hardly a valley that doesn't have several families who have been helped by the generosity of our supporters and the love and dedication of CAP's employees and volunteers.

God continues to bring us people in need. Not long ago, a beat-up old Chevrolet belching smoke pulled into my driveway. A man came out of the car and as he walked toward me, I saw the hopeful faces of five small children pressed against the car windows. He told me his car was on its last legs, his family had nowhere to stay, and they had no money for food. They had no relatives in the area to whom they could turn. The oldest boy got out of the car and came over to where we were talking. "Is the man going to give us food? We are so hungry," he said to his father.

The man's face was red with embarrassment and shame as his son related their need. He wondered if I could give them a little food and gasoline so they could drive to Florida where he had relatives.

I said, "Get back in the car and follow me. I'm going to take you to a special place."

Just a few weeks earlier, we had put the final touches on our Good Samaritan Home, a temporary shelter where we hope to help homeless families get back on their feet. We drove over there and the two CAP volunteers who run the Good Samaritan Home took the family in hand.

I came back a few hours later to check on them and the transformation was astonishing. The children had all bathed and their clothes were washed. The father and mother were smiling, watching their kids eat their first good meal in days.

The family stayed with us a few days while we helped them get their car fixed. We loaned them enough money for gas, and they were soon on their way to make a new start in Florida.

I am very excited about this Good Samaritan Home. The Good Samaritan has always been my favorite of Jesus' parables.

Some years ago, I received a commendation called the Good Samaritan Award. I was touched because only two years earlier Mother Teresa of Calcutta had won the same award. I don't belong there, but it was an honor to be put in the same group as her.

The Good Samaritan Award is a beautiful hand-carving of that famous pilgrim helping a wounded man by the side of the road. For years, I had the carving on the desk in my office.

When the Good Samaritan Home opened, I put the carving on its mantel as a reminder to the people of CAP to be Good Samaritans. It's a reminder that we are bound to those we help, not by poverty and not by need, but by love.

It's funny, I think of that Good Samaritan Award even more now that it is not on my desk. Somehow, its absence reminds me that it's not enough to have helped someone once, or even twice. A true Good

Samaritan never stops helping. My prayer each day
is that I will never think of my neighbor as someone
who is poor or disabled or old or sick. I hope I can
think of them instead as Christ does, as a wonderful
brother or sister in need of a friend on the sometimes
difficult pilgrimage of life.

Lighting Candles Along the Trail

Throughout the ages, pilgrims brought the learning of their countries to foreign lands and brought back the learning of distant peoples. They carried candles of knowledge to and from distant lands to light the darkness with wisdom.

When I visited my old house in Berea, I remembered the series of events that led me to understand that I should do the same thing in my own pilgrimage.

I remembered the day when a woman came to me just before Christmas. She told me her husband had left her several years before and she was trying to raise three young children by herself. She had a serious illness and needed an operation that would require a long recovery. She didn't know what to do with her three young children. She knew she would be unable to meet their needs for a long time.

I told her I would see what I could do. That night I called my sister, who was a nun in an orphanage in Northern Kentucky. I told her the children needed a home for a while, but we couldn't afford to pay for their care. Thank goodness, the Sisters generously agreed to take the children. A week before Christmas, they kissed their mother goodbye and I drove away with three teary-eyed kids.

When we got near Lexington, Kentucky, where there were houses along the road, the children marveled at all the colored Christmas lights. A little voice spoke from the back seat, "Father, did something happen? Did somebody get hurt? Is that why they have all those lights?"

I explained that the lights were for Christmas — a way of celebrating the birth of Jesus. The children were silent with awe. They had never seen Christmas decorations before. The Christmas they had at the orphanage was the first one they'd ever had with a tree and presents.

In the meantime, I found their mother a place to live while she recuperated. She recovered from her illness and surgery and found a pretty good job. When the kids came back home to her, they were a very happy family.

Seeing those kids and the way they had been isolated and the lack of knowledge they had about the world, made me realize that if I were to truly make changes in Appalachia, I had to work with children. Ideas of how to do this rattled around in my brain for quite a while.

The next memory that came to me as I stood in my old driveway in Berea was of Bobtown, a little dot on the map that will always hold a special place in my heart. I had gotten into a rhythm of making frequent runs up to my parents' home to pick up car loads of clothes and food. Coming south to Berea at night, I would always be tired and thinking of bed. Bobtown was the last town before Berea and there were two big peaks there. When I saw those twin peaks against the night sky, I knew I was almost home.

On one of those trips I came to a fork in the road of my pilgrimage. In Bobtown, with the twin peaks in sight, the idea that would later become the Christian Appalachian Project was born.

I was feeling pretty good that night because I had a full load of donated supplies, but I was very tired and looking forward to sleep.

When I saw the twin peaks of Bobtown, I prayed, "Thank you, Lord, for keeping me awake and safe on this trip and helping me to bring these things for the poor."

But my next thought was "Big deal. What good are you doing? How much are you accomplishing? You're just a truck driver."

Now there is nothing wrong with being a truck driver, of course, but I realized that being a truck driver was not what I was meant to do in Appalachia. Driving back and forth every week with a load of food and clothes would not solve anything. Poverty would continue. The clothes would wear out and the food would be eaten, and the people would have the same problems they started with.

I remembered some things I'd read about other people who had fought poverty in other places and I knew that I had to do something more. All I was doing was feeding people while they suffered in the shackles of poverty. I had to find a way to help people break those shackles.

Tired as I was, I couldn't sleep when I got home that night. I began thinking of all the things I could do. The list went on and on. But the two things that kept coming back to the top of that list were: that I had to do something for the children and I had to do something about education.

I was convinced that those were the keys.

The plans and dreams I made that night were the real beginnings of the Christian Appalachian Project. It was as if, for the first time, I had a map to tell me which way to go on my pilgrimage.

By this time, I had begun to work in Lancaster, Kentucky, 22 miles or so to the west of Berea. There is a lake nearby, making it a great place for a summer camp for kids. I thought that a camp would be the perfect way to get kids out of the hollers for a little while and show them other ways to live and grow.

As I mentioned earlier, the day after I prayed about this dream, a realtor showed me some property on a lake near Lancaster, and we were on our way.

Even before we had signed the papers, I had an architect-friend drive out to the property. I told him about my dream and that I needed a special building with a big kitchen, a dining area, and bunk rooms for 20-25 kids. He went to work designing something, but I was so anxious to start the camp that I didn't want to let another summer go by. We bought a used trailer home for $400, set it up on the property, and rounded up eight needy kids.

My associate, Father Leo Sudcamp, and I did everything: the cooking, the swimming lessons, the arts and crafts. We were only able to have two or three one-week sessions because we ran out of money, but the kids who came had a great time and they spread the word far and wide.

The new camp building was finished in time for the next summer, and we were able to take in more kids. Each year, we built another building until at the end of about five years we were taking 50 kids per week.

It was wonderful for the kids to be on their own, away from their parents and learning new things. I'll never forget one boy named Lucien.

We kept telling Lucien that he needed to take a shower, but he just wouldn't do it. Finally, I said, "Maybe Lucien doesn't know what a shower is." We explained it to him.

"You go into the shower section of the bathroom, turn the water on, and soap yourself all over and then rinse off. That's all there is to it."

Well that's what Lucien did, but we forgot one important step. We didn't tell him to take his clothes off first. He took a shower fully dressed.

We had a good-natured laugh with him and he did get the hang of showering before he left the camp, but it showed us just how little some of these kids knew about the world outside.

There were other kids who had to be shown how to use a faucet and a toilet. They had never seen indoor plumbing. When they saw that they could get water out of a faucet and didn't need to haul it up from the bottom of a well, they were so excited. It was like Christmas in July.

Wonderful volunteers began to come to the camp to share their experiences and their wisdom and their knowledge with the kids. They helped the children learn to dream — to imagine that their own pilgrimages could range far wider than just their own holler. It's hard to believe just how much this exposure to new ideas affected the kids. I can't count the number of people who still come up to me and say, "Father, I was at your camp when I was a kid and I want you to know that those few weeks changed my life."

It wasn't just the children who were affected, either. Many of the volunteers came away from our camps with new goals for their own pilgrimages.

The more I saw how much this camp meant to the kids and the volunteers, the more I worried about it. After all, I wasn't sure how long I'd be in Appalachia. I wanted to stay, but the Church might, at any moment, decide to assign me elsewhere. The tradition was that priests didn't stay long in eastern

Kentucky. It was like being banished to Siberia. After a while, you'd receive a pardon and get released to a more pleasant place.

Personally, I couldn't imagine a better place to do God's work, but since I couldn't control my fate in that regard, I wanted to make sure the camp would continue if I were reassigned.

I spoke with Bishop Ackerman, my superior, and we agreed that the camp, Cliffview, should become an entity separate from the Church so it could continue no matter which priest was assigned to that area. There was a cliff across the lake from our camp, so we incorporated the camp as Cliffview Lodge.

In looking back on this pilgrimage, I know that was a very big step. It was the first time we realized that fighting poverty and changing the lives of the people of Appalachia was a job too big for even the Catholic Church. We had to open this journey to all who wanted to help. We had to let go in order to grow.

We had to create a new organization that could carry on the Church's mission of love for the poor, caring for the underprivileged, and moral commitment to God's virtues.

That was a very big step, the first time such a thing had been done in eastern Kentucky and probably in all of Appalachia. It was the first baby step towards the interdenominational organization we now call the Christian Appalachian Project.

Over the years, we've expanded our camps, now

hosting more than 1,300 kids every summer. We're still teaching kids to dream.

This past summer we had a young boy named Timmy at CAP's Camp Andrew Jackson. He has a difficult family life and had withdrawn into a shell of fear and self-doubt. Whenever we suggested he try something new, he'd say, "I can't do that." For the first two days it was all we heard from him.

After a week of the counselor's encouragement, little by little, he saw that he could accomplish something, and began to change his tune.

Timmy was a star on skit night. He made up a story and performed it for about ninety people, all mesmerized. When it was over, Timmy was beaming.

By the end of the week, instead of saying, "I can't do that," Timmy would say, "I'll try it and see what happens." Now that's not exactly overflowing confidence, but it's a start.

That's the way I felt about our camps, back in the early days. They were a start — a good start — but only a start. Getting to know the kids who came to Cliffview convinced me, more strongly than ever, that education also had to be a major focus of our efforts. I was dismayed that many eight-, nine-, and ten-year-olds couldn't read, for example. I'd say "Go stand over there, near the sign that says, 'Wash your hands before eating,'" and they'd look at me blankly.

Even young adults often didn't know how to read. I hired a young man named Estill to do various jobs, including driving. The car he was using needed a few things done to it, and I handed him the owner's manual from the glove compartment. "Here," I said, "It tells you right here what needs to be done."

Estill looked at me, sighed and said, "Maybe it would be better if you told me what to do."

I was puzzled because he knew I was in a hurry and had to leave. Then it dawned on me. "Estill," I said, "Can't you read this?"

He lowered his head and looked at his shoes. "No. I can't read much at all."

The terrible thing is that he had a high school diploma. I still don't know how he got it. He was an excellent athlete and the star of his school's football team and I suppose they let him through. What a tragedy. His football skills were useless to him once he graduated, but the fact that he couldn't read would enslave him for the rest of his life.

At least he went through the motions of finishing high school. So many children never even do that. I was invited to speak at a high school graduation where about 50 kids were getting diplomas. Before the ceremony, one of the teachers gave me a tour of the school. I asked her, "How many students were in this class in the beginning, as freshmen?"

Her answer shocked me. There had been 150 students at the beginning — only 50 finished.

This lack of education cripples the entire area. Over the years, I have tried to convince businesses to relocate here in Appalachia, but I hear the same thing over and over.

"We can't locate there because so many people in the workforce are unskilled and uneducated."

In my own life, education was stressed from the very first. It was portrayed as a lifelong goal, not something you did for a few years in school. My grandfather taught me that. He didn't have a lot of formal education, but he was determined to learn. He read constantly and he always chose difficult reading because he wanted to improve his understanding.

Even today, the last thing I do every evening before I turn out the lights is read. I'm still trying to follow my grandfather's example, trying to educate myself.

We've tried to create education programs for every age, from 2 months to 90 years. We created preschool programs for the children of poverty long before the federal government began the Head Start program. We now have six child development centers, where we help preschoolers get a good start before they head off to public schools for first grade.

We built a special school called the Mountain Christian Academy. At this school for preschool through twelfth grades, we provide an excellent education at low, or even no, cost for children from very poor families. The school is interdenominational, with children from several different religious backgrounds, but it is a school that teaches Christian values. We remind the kids every day that God loves them. This school is something of which I'm very proud.

We have built teen centers where we welcome young people to come together to share activities and grow. The staff at these centers are wonderful volunteers and qualified local people who serve as the role models that are often missing in the lives of kids who grow up in poverty.

There is a young girl named Cheryl who truly benefited from this attention recently. Cheryl was very withdrawn, and at first wouldn't talk to anyone at the teen center — not even the other kids. She sat in the corner by herself, but kept coming, day after day. Linda, one of our volunteers, felt that Cheryl must be looking for something. Each day, when she drove Cheryl home, Linda talked to her. At first, Cheryl just grunted acknowledgment. Sometimes she'd say a simple "yes" or "no," but after several weeks, she began to open up. She was talking in sentences and then whole paragraphs.

Eventually, Cheryl and Linda became great friends and the young girl chattered in the car all the way from the teen center to her home. She began talking to Linda about her dreams and hopes, and listened when Linda made suggestions about new possibilities.

She began interacting with the other teens and the other volunteers at the center. She began trying new activities at school.

All of this happened because, for the first time in her life, Cheryl had the attention of a concerned adult.

Once we had created education programs for children, we knew we had to do something to help the many illiterate and poorly educated adults.

We began offering programs to help people study for general equivalency diplomas (GED) for high school. We also offered literacy classes for people who could not read at all.

With the isolation of many communities, however, we knew we were not reaching as far as we could. There were so many people who couldn't come to our classes because of the distance and the lack of transportation. We trained teachers to go out into their communities and teach others. This led to our School on Wheels. Then we took that one step further and fixed up an old school bus as a mobile classroom. It has a bathroom, desks, blackboards, and computers run by a generator. We call it the Little Red School Bus. I was really pleased when National Geographic pictured it in an article on Appalachia.

We now have two of these Little Red School Buses, and just last week I visited one, accompanied by reporters from the Cable News Network. We met with Mary, one of our teachers, and two of her students. After we talked, Mary asked me to visit the home of two students, a woman and her 18 year old son. Before the School Bus began coming to her home, the woman didn't even know the letters of the alphabet.

I got directions to the woman's home and followed a dirt road that ended at the mouth of a holler. As I

walked up the steps to the front porch, the woman
ran towards me. She said she had just returned home
and found her husband lying on the floor, unable to
speak.

We called for an ambulance and they soon
appeared. After examining him, the paramedics
decided he needed oxygen. They went to the ambulance and returned with an oxygen tank, but the valve
was stuck and they couldn't move it. In the meantime, the man on the floor still could not speak and
appeared to be failing.

I ran out to my car and found a wrench in the trunk.
With the wrench I was able to open the valve and the
lifesaving oxygen flowed. We got the man onto a
stretcher and into the ambulance. The doors were shut
and the ambulance sped away, carrying him to the
hospital in the next county.

I later received word through Mary that the woman
was extremely grateful for my help. She said her
husband had suffered a stroke and that his doctor
told her that without oxygen, he would have died.

In this instance, the Little Red School Bus not only
gave that woman and her son pride by guiding them
into a world of knowledge, but it also helped to save
a life.

It's amazing the many roads our Lord has led me
down on this pilgrimage.

It's also rewarding to see what our education efforts
have meant to the people we serve. I am especially
pleased to see how many older people have over-

come embarrassment and pride to say, "I want to read." The desire for learning is so strong.

Willie is one of those people. He was 66 when he decided he wanted to learn to read. Can you imagine the courage it must have taken for him to do that?

When Willie was a child growing up in the '30s and '40s, he had little time for school. He worked his family's farm and when he was old enough, he did what so many young Appalachian men did in those days, he joined his father in the coal mines. But Willie knew the value of education and what he was missing. When his little brother tried to skip school, Willie would chase the boy to school with a switch.

Willie's brother got good grades and eventually had a good career. Willie worked in the coal mines most of his life.

Now Willie is retired and he wants to learn to read.

He's been at it for about three years, working hard with CAP tutors. His goal is to learn to read the Bible by himself.

"The first thing I ever read by myself was the Lord's Prayer!" he exclaims.

It's never too late for someone like Willie to open the doors of reading and education. And it's not too late for us to open the doors of reading and education for Appalachia. One person at a time, CAP is helping to reduce the illiteracy rate and build up the educational level of the whole region.

We're doing this, in part, so Appalachia will be

more attractive for businesses wanting to relocate. But education is its own reward. It's a kind of freedom.

When I talk to children and adults about education, I don't tell them that it will get them a better job, or allow them to own a better house. I tell them that Jesus said, "The truth will set you free." Education will allow you to be the special person God meant you to be, I tell them. It will allow you to reach to the stars. It will allow you to dream, to help others, and to build a better Appalachia.

When you educate yourself as much as possible, you become one of those candles of light along the trail of our pilgrimage.

That's the way I think of our camps, child development centers, and adult education programs. As the CAP family journeys down the road of this wonderful pilgrimage, we carry candles of wisdom and education and we stop to light the candles of others along the way. When all those candles shine together, we'll be a procession that can continue in any darkness and against any obstacle until we reach our goal.

Recruiting Other Pilgrims

Sometimes, when a pilgrim of old stopped along his route and told stories, his tales and his dreams excited others to join him. "Wait up," they said. "We want to come too."

I thank God that I have had the same experience in my life and that He has brought so many volunteers to help me in my work. When I walked around the neighborhood in Berea, and saw the old barn we renovated, it reminded me of all the pilgrims who have joined me on my voyage — all the volunteers who, over the course of 45 years, have said, "Wait up. We want to come too."

That old barn in Berea was one of our first quarters for volunteers. When the numbers grew and volunteers worked in four counties, we held Sunday night meetings in the yard of the barn to bring the volunteers together once a week. They pretended to hate those meetings. For a while, they prayed for rain every Sunday. But since I held the meetings, rain or shine, they finally stopped asking for bad weather.

At the meeting, each group of volunteers talked about what they had done the week before, and what they planned to do in the week ahead, and what their dreams were for the future. We put our heads together to solve problems or figure out a new opportunity to help people in need. We'd end the meeting with prayers and songs. The volunteers may have prayed for rain, but they always left those meetings with a song on their lips and hope in their hearts.

After I was ordained a priest in June of 1949, I spent a week with my family and then went on a retreat to the Trappist Monastery at Gethsemane, Kentucky. An old Trappist Brother from Italy showed me to my room. The kind Brother must have sensed that I was feeling a bit uneasy and out of place. Before he left me to unpack my belongings, he said "You pray for me and I'll pray for you and both of us will be better."

His words came back to me when I was again feeling alone and out of place during those first days in Berea. As long as we help each other we are never alone. The journey will always go faster and better with someone walking by your side.

In those early days, I often wondered how I could ever face the monumental task ahead of me. I could not turn away, but how could I ever complete all that God was calling me to do?

God's wisdom told me, "Don't worry about the end. Just be concerned about today. And don't be afraid to ask for help." His infinite wisdom brought many wonderful people into my life to join me in my journey.

Oftentimes, I didn't even need to ask for help — people offered to help. For example, the first Sunday that I was in Appalachia, I went to say Mass at the church in Richmond, Kentucky, because we did not yet have a place in Berea. After the services were over, a gentleman came to me and said he was the business manager of the local newspaper. "I know you are going to need some help," he said. "I don't know how much experience you have in finances but I'm willing to give you all the time you need. I'll keep your books and do whatever else I can."

I thought to myself, "What a wonderful gesture. If I only *had* some finances, I could put him to work." Nonetheless, I was thrilled to have the man offer to join me.

A week later, a man from Berea, Bill Watson, came to my house. He was a salesman for a wholesale grocery company and he traveled throughout the mountain area. He said, "Father, whatever you need and I have, it's yours. I have a pick-up truck, and if you need to haul things, you let me know."

I took him up on that offer many times. He was always ready to drop whatever he was doing and come to my aid with quiet dignity and generosity.

Not long after that, a wonderful woman named Lila Murphy offered her assistance. I had met her when her husband was dying. Lila was not Catholic, but her husband was. He hadn't been able to go to church for many years because there was no church within 30 miles. When it looked as if he had only a few days left, Lila called me and asked if I would come and help him meet his God.

Later, I conducted his funeral. After the funeral was over, Lila said, "I was so impressed by this service and the things you said today. I want to know more about it myself." A few months later I baptized her as a new Catholic. She was 80 years old.

That wasn't enough for Lila though. She said, "Now I want to start doing something worthwhile with my life."

Lila had raised her four nieces and nephews after her sister died. She was an energetic force in her community. It seemed to me she had already done lots of worthwhile things in her life. But she wasn't satisfied. She felt called to rescue this poor young priest who was wandering like a fool through the hills. So she became my housekeeper in Berea. She worked beside me off and on until she was in her 90s. I can still hear her saying, "What's needed to be done next?"

Younger people joined me as fellow pilgrims. Before I came to Appalachia, I taught a year of high school in Newport, Kentucky. Not long after I moved to Appalachia, a group of my former students came during the summer to help paint, repair buildings, cut grass — all kinds of things. They were the first of tens of thousands of young men and women who gave their summers and school vacations to join this journey through the Holy Land of Appalachia.

Religious people began to come. At first, they were Catholics like me — nuns, priests, and brothers from as close as Lexington, Kentucky, and as far away as New Hampshire. Eventually, ministers from other faiths came as well. Many of them gave up their week or two of vacation each year to come and help preach and work with me in the mountains.

My own family became my most dependable volunteers. No request was too big. My brothers and sisters came with their spouses and friends. They helped me build churches and camps and fix up rummage stores.

My parents were always there, whenever I needed them. I'll never forget the summer that my father worked on crutches. His leg had been crushed in a serious construction accident, and he was out of work for 9 months. He insisted on helping me put up a new camp building, though. I can still see him limping around on those crutches, supervising the work and pitching in wherever he could. It made me proud to be his son.

My mother helped as well. She spent over a year and a half managing our rummage store in Mt. Vernon and doing whatever else needed to be done. But her most generous act was the one she made when she was dying.

She was in the hospital, terribly ill with bone cancer and in excruciating pain. The nurses asked her, "Mrs. Beiting why don't you scream? Why don't you yell?

Why don't you do something to relieve your pain?"

She looked at them and said, "No. I am offering up this pain for my son and the work that goes on in the mountains. Through my suffering, I can ask God's blessing upon them."

When she had only a few days to live, we brought her home from the hospital. Before she died, she told my sisters to gather up all her belongings and sell them in a yard sale on her front lawn and give the money to my work in the mountains.

When I prayed with her for the last time, she asked that all of her family love God and serve Him and His church. To the very end, she was a volunteer.

It is impossible to put a value on what volunteers have meant on this journey. When I think back, I can see so many of the faces of those who walked with me. Some have been walking beside me for decades. Others came, held my hand for a little while, and went away again. All of them have helped build this family of faith and helped make the load a little lighter to carry.

One of the things that amazes me about many volunteers is that, unlike me, they know they won't be around to see the end result of their projects. Some people came, for example, and helped us put up camp buildings, knowing they wouldn't be able to return the next summer to see the kids enjoy the camp.

It takes a lot of faith to give your heart and sweat to a dream, knowing that you won't be there so see the dream come true.

I often wonder what keeps these people coming from all over the country, and even from foreign countries, to join this pilgrimage. When I ask them, they look at me as if I'm crazy. "Why Father, we get far more than we give," they say. "You should know that."

Just a few weeks ago, I had a visit from a woman who was a volunteer with us 27 years ago when she was just 16. She was only with us for three weeks, but she was so moved by that experience that when she went home, she continued to help the poor in her own community. She made sure the man she married had similar ideals.

She returned after all these years because those three short weeks were one of the highlights of her life and she wanted her husband and her children to meet me and see what she had helped to build. We spent three or four hours at my kitchen table one Sunday after church, reminiscing about the early days, and it was clear to me and to her family that she had received far more than she gave — which was a lot.

Not long ago, I got a call from our Congressional Representative in Washington, Mr. Harold Rogers. He said, "I didn't know you had friends in such high places."

"What do you mean?" I asked.

"There was a gentleman here yesterday who asked me if I knew where Rockcastle County, Kentucky, was. I told him I did, of course, and I wondered how he knew of it.

"He told me he spent a summer there working with Father Beiting and the Christian Appalachian Project. And he told me it was a summer that changed his life."

"Who was it?" I asked.

"James Louis Freeh, head of the FBI."

Well, it's nice to know I have a friend in a high place if I ever get into trouble with the law. But it's even nicer to know that we've provided an opportunity for so many people to have the wonderful experience of giving of themselves.

There's nothing like it.

Beyond that wonderful feeling that comes from giving, I believe volunteering offers the chance to see Jesus in action every day, and to help Him as well. Our Lord said, "As long as you did it to one of these, the least of my brothers and sisters, you did it unto Me." When our volunteers visit with an elderly woman who needs a friend, they are visiting Jesus. When they hold the hand of a small child at a child development center, they are holding the hand of Jesus. When they teach an old man to read, they are teaching their Savior.

As this pilgrimage goes on, people keep joining us. I hope it will always be so. In fact, I hope even more will join us in the coming years. There is so much left to do.

I especially urge older people to join us. In the early days, when Bill Watson and Lila Murphy and others like them were offering their help, mostly adults and senior citizens joined me. Then, for a long time, it was mostly young people. In recent years, it's been swinging back towards older folks and I think that's wonderful.

Nothing can replace the energy and enthusiasm of the young. But nothing can compare to the wisdom and patience of older people either.

These days, more and more of our volunteers are over the age of 50. They have many different reasons for making a change in their lives at that age. Sometimes the death of a spouse leaves a void that we can help fill with purpose, friendship, and love. Others are dissatisfied with their careers and want to find a way to live a more spiritual life with more meaningful work. Still others have retired early, since so many companies have downsized in the last five years. They're too young to sit around, and they have the freedom to come here and offer something back to God.

Most of all I think older people have vision that is not available to the young. They know that God needs to be a part of each and every life. They know that without God, there is no destination for their pilgrimages.

I think they realize that if this land is to become a land of promise once again, it will not be because of what politicians do, but because of what people who have benefited from this country are willing to give back. Change comes only from people.

I think of the wonderful couple who live and work at the Good Samaritan Home, our new temporary home for homeless families. This couple is retired and have already raised a family. They both had professional careers, he as a banker and she as a nurse. This could be their time to relax, but they feel they still have much to give to the world. They have love and wisdom to give to children and young couples. Now, they share their lives with other families, helping them to learn how to better manage their lives.

Like them, many senior citizens are unwilling to sit on the side and watch the pilgrimage pass them by in their golden years. They have too much of God's life and love inside them for that. They know their journey is not over until the Lord calls them home.

There has been too much emphasis on the weaknesses of age and not enough on the benefits. This robs our senior citizens of their dignity and their destiny. When I talk to older people, they say, "Look, I'm far from dead. I understand things about life that these young people can't possibly know. I'm far from being a discarded item in the American landscape. I want to be a part of the new beginning."

I, myself, feel a deep sense of pride to be among their number. The next ten years are going to see a greater and greater number of people over 50 stepping forward to say, "Lord, here I am. Send me to do Your work."

I welcome them and I want them to know that there is a need and a place for them here in Appalachia. I say to them what the poet Robert Browning said to his wife Elizabeth, "Grow old alone with me. The best is yet to be."

As I grow older myself, I know I have to open up this pilgrimage to others. There are so many who could join us and walk with us towards our goal. The goal itself is not even as important as the journey with friends. When all is said and done, the most beautiful thing God ever made was people. And people are at their most beautiful when they are volunteers — giving freely of their unique gifts.

That's when they reflect the face of God.

Every night before I sleep, I think of our volunteers, and I often say the following prayer:

Heavenly Father, I ask your blessing upon the good and wonderful people who have entered my life. Dear Lord, could you go *before* each and every one of them, that you might lead them and guide them on their way through life. Lord could you also come *behind* them that you might guard them and protect them from every danger and from all harm. Lord could you also come and hover *above* them that you might rain down on them your many blessings, your richest gifts. But more than anything Lord, could you come and live *within* their hearts that you might fill them with your joy and with your peace.

To all the volunteers who have walked with me on this pilgrimage through the Holy Land of Appalachia, I say, until we meet again, wherever you go, whatever you do, my prayer is always the same, may you go with God.

When I first came to the mountains, one of my biggest challenges was overcoming people's suspicions about Catholic priests.

So much has changed -- yet so much remains the same. Home visitations continue to be a major part of my ministry.

Here I am surveying property for CAP's programs -- an act of faith!

PHOTO: CAP ARCHIVES

CHRISTIAN APPALACHIAN PROJECT
25 YEARS AND GROWING!

PHOTO: CAP ARCHIVES

In 1989, CAP celebrated 25 years of service to the poor of Appalachia.

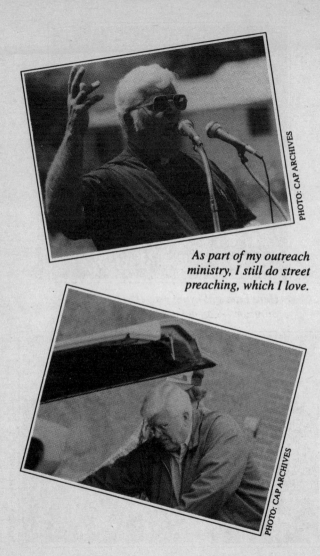

As part of my outreach ministry, I still do street preaching, which I love.

Getting the jalopy ready to take God's show on the road.

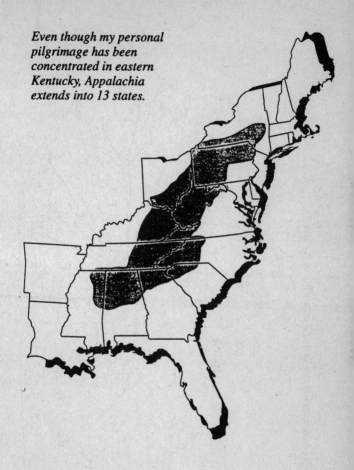

Even though my personal pilgrimage has been concentrated in eastern Kentucky, Appalachia extends into 13 states.

CAP's work spans the entire Appalachian region -- which extends from a portion of New York State to Mississippi.

My street preaching has carried me into 17 counties in Kentucky.

MAP: FR. RALPH BEITING

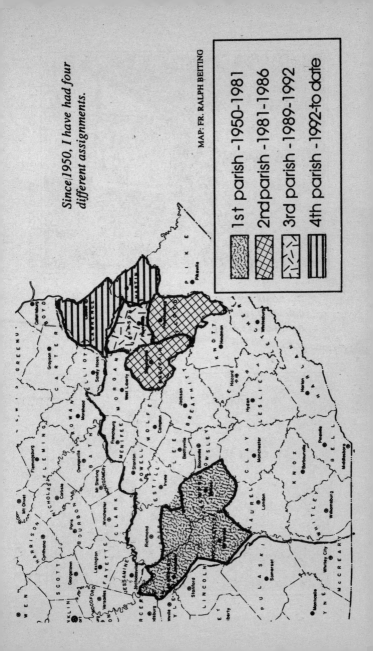

Since 1950, I have had four different assignments.

MAP: FR. RALPH BEITING

1st parish - 1950-1981

2nd parish - 1981-1986

3rd parish - 1989-1992

4th parish - 1992-to date

Burnouts are a common occurrence in Appalachia as a result of woodburning stoves and antiquated wiring.

For many families in Appalachia, CAP's Christmas Basket Program is the highlight of the year.

CAP's child development centers help children get off on the right foot before entering school.

Walking With the Wise Ones

When I was finally able to tear myself away from reminiscing at the old house in Berea, I drove out to see a place down the road that holds a very dear spot in my heart. It's called the Emmaus Christian Life Center. We created this special home for senior citizens in 1982 to fulfill a dream I have had ever since I began this pilgrimage in the mountains 45 years ago.

When I first came here, I soon discovered what all pilgrims discover — road maps and guide books aren't enough. If you really want to reach your goal, you have to find someone who has been down the same roads. It didn't take me long to learn two things here in Appalachia — first, that older people are often those in the greatest need, and second, they have an enormous store of knowledge and wisdom about their problems and the problems of all those who live in poverty.

They were the ones who knew the roads I should travel on my pilgrimage. And they have helped me so much on my journey.

In fact, if it weren't for the aid of a wonderful older woman, we never would have been able to create the Emmaus Center.

The Emmaus Center used to be a motel. When the new interstate was put in a couple of miles west of Berea, the motel was no longer on the main route, and its business fell off sharply. Every time I drove by it, I thought how it could be so much more useful as a home for senior citizens than as a decaying, underused motel. The man who owned it, however, refused to sell.

Then he made the mistake of telling his mother that I was interested in buying the property. His mother looked him in the eyes, with a look that only a mother can give, and she said, "Father Beiting came and visited me when I was very sick not long ago and no one else seemed to care. He was wonderfully kind to me. So I want you to do whatever you can to help him. If he wants that motel, you sell it to him."

He sold us the motel, and at a pretty good price, too.

Now, instead of sitting empty most of the year, it is filled with senior citizens who need special attention, but who are not ill enough to be in a nursing home. At the Emmaus Center, they are safe and they get the medical attention they need, but they still have the freedom many older people are afraid of losing when they are forced to go to a nursing home.

I think the people I most enjoy helping are the

senior citizens because they are so grateful, and they have so much to offer in return.

As I drove around Berea, thinking about all the wonderful people I'd known there, I passed the road where Mrs. Hamilton used to live.

Mrs. Hamilton and her husband were both Catholic, and they had 11 children. But because there were no Catholic churches within 40 or 50 miles, they were unable to go to a Catholic service for many, many years. As the children grew up, they joined various local churches.

When I first began to have services in Berea, Mrs. Hamilton was always there. I got to know this wonderful woman and her story. She told me that her husband worked for the railroad and they had relocated to Berea many years before. She also told me that her husband had died a few years back and all the children were grown and gone. It was a struggle for her to make it to church every Sunday but she said, "I haven't been able to go to Mass for so long. Now I want to make up for it."

Then I didn't see her for a few Sundays in a row. I was afraid something was wrong, so I went to her house and found it empty. It was obvious no one had been there for a while. I was quite concerned, but I didn't know how to check on her.

The next Sunday, I got a call from one of her sons who lived in Cincinnati. He told me his mother was very sick and she was staying with his sister just outside of Berea. He asked me to go and see her because she was anxious to make a confession and receive communion before she died.

Then he said, "Don't tell my brothers and sisters I told you to go there. They don't want to have anything to do with you, and they're mad that Ma keeps asking for you."

I went out to the house the next day. It was an awful day, rainy and cold. I had to walk through the rain across a field for two hundred feet or so to reach the house.

Two of Mrs. Hamilton's sons were standing on the porch. They had obviously seen me coming across the field and they were waiting for me.

"You might as well turn around and go back. We don't want a Catholic priest here," one of them said. "We don't want anything to do with you. Nobody wants you here."

I said, "Do you mind if we talk on the porch? I'm getting soaked here in the rain."

The other son said, "Oh, let him come up on the porch. He can't do any harm out here."

They let me on the porch, out of the rain, but they insisted that I was not wanted or needed.

"Well, let me ask you a question," I said, "When you die and you go before the Lord, which of you is going to have the nerve to tell Him you refused your mother's last request?" I was being hard on them, but I knew they were making a mistake and I had to stop them.

"After that woman gave you birth, nursed you, fed

you, and raised you, are you going to tell God that you wouldn't let her have what she wanted at the end of her life?

"Which one of you has the nerve to do that?"

They both looked down and there was silence. Finally, the younger of the two said, "Man, I don't want to do that."

"He's trying to trick us," the other said.

"No, I'm not trying to trick you. I just want to make sure you know what you're doing."

The younger one said, "Let him go in. He can't do any harm."

"Fine," the older one said, "But you try one Catholic thing in there, and out you go."

I went in, not sure just what was going to happen since I certainly was intending to do "Catholic things."

I walked through a room full of relatives and found Mrs. Hamilton in a bedroom surrounded by another five or six of her children and in-laws. When I entered the room, Mrs. Hamilton's eyes lit up. "Oh, I am so glad you came," she told me. "I need you so much."

Mrs. Hamilton told me she wanted to confess her sins, so I asked if everyone would step out of the room for a few minutes and give us privacy. The daughter insisted that everyone stay. I told Mrs. Hamilton that, under those circumstances, she didn't have to say all her sins in public, she could just tell me she was sorry for them.

She looked at her daughter and the others in the

room and she said, "Father, this is my last confession and I'm going to make it a good one. If they don't want to leave, then let them hear what I have to say."

She made her confession and I gave her absolution. Then I read from the Bible, anointed her with oils, and did other "Catholic" things like giving her the Body of Christ in Communion.

When I left her, the younger of the two brothers who had met me on the porch earlier, followed me out the door.

He grabbed my arm and said, "Hey. That wasn't as bad as we thought it was going to be. You even read from the Bible. I guess we're glad you came."

Mrs. Hamilton died a few days later and I said her funeral Mass. All her sons and daughters were there. They were still a little uncomfortable with all those "Catholic" things, but I think they felt better that their mother had received her last wishes.

I think it was incredibly wise of her to leave them with one final lesson. With her last ounces of strength, she taught them a lesson in tolerance and understanding for people of different faiths, a beautiful tribute to her life as a mother and a teacher of her children.

When I began this pilgrimage 45 years ago, I was 26 years of age. Now I am 71. By any calculation I am one of those older people now. I look at pictures of that slim young man of 26 and then I look in the mirror and see my white hair and enlarged torso and I know full well that 45 years have passed. A blood

clot behind my left eye makes seeing, and therefore
driving, difficult. Arthritis is a constant bother. Sometimes it's my hands, sometimes it's my elbow, it's
always my left knee. I can't walk straight any more.
I have diabetes, and the effects of several automobile accidents cause me daily discomforts. I can't run
very fast. In fact, some young folks joke that what I
do is not even a run at all, it's sort of a lope.

Worst of all, when I sit down in my house after a
weary day, it isn't long before I begin to doze. I used
to have endless energy.

Sometimes I say to myself, "It's tough to get old. I
wish I were 40 again."

Then I remember what I said to a woman I once
visited in a hospital. She was in her 90s. When I entered her room, I reached out and held her hand and
she looked at me and said, "Father can you tell me in
the name of all that is holy, what good is a 95 year
old woman? I'm a burden and a trouble to everyone."

I thought for a moment and I said, "You aren't looking at your worth and value. You're only looking at
the tasks you are performing. Your value to God and
this world is every bit the same as it ever was. You're
being asked to take on a different task, that's all. You
are being asked to suffer. This is the hard part of life,
and God wants to know if you have the courage to
accept this part. Youth was easy because you were in
charge. Now God wants to know if you'll let Him
run the show."

I have met many travelers along the way who were old when I met them or who have grown old with me. Some have been poor, neglected, and lonely. Others had been abused by people who had taken advantage of them. Still others were living out their final years in quiet desperation. I knew we needed to reach out and touch them and do as much for them as we possibly could.

We fixed their homes, brought them indoor plumbing, and built them bathrooms. We patched leaky roofs and insulated their old houses to keep out the cold. We brought hot meals and warm clothing. We brought medical assistance. We wrote letters and read the news. We read the Bible and prayed. When they were too frail to live alone, we found them places where they could be cared for with love. The best thing we gave was a friendly ear. We listened and learned as they passed on the wisdom gained from a difficult life in the mountains. We assured them of their usefulness and purpose in life.

And whenever we have done these things, we have been showered with gratitude and prayers. But even more importantly, we have benefited enormously from their knowledge and love.

Now that I am old, I understand the three greatest fears that plague older pilgrims: they don't want to be a burden, they don't want to be useless, and they don't want young people to take advantage of them.

I understand these fears all too well.

The first, and possibly the deepest, fear is of

burdening others. When my father had to be taken to a nursing home, he was very depressed. He had always been strong and kept saying to all of us. "I don't want to be a burden. I don't want to weigh you all down."

I sat at his bedside and said "Dad, you're giving us an opportunity to pay you back for the love, the time, and the devotion you gave to us."

How many nights had he and my mother stood at our bedsides and brought us through illness? How many times had he taken the time to teach us to play ball, drive a car, or plow a field? He was no more burden to us than we had been to him. Now he was allowing us the opportunity to thank him.

His purpose in our lives was greater now than when he was strong and did all the giving.

There were other benefits. One of my nieces said about my sister, "Mom taught us how children should act by the way she cared for her father and mother." We were showing the next generation an example of the eternal power of love.

I don't know if I ever made my father understand that he was no burden to us, but I do know that he made it possible for me to realize that truth. As I approach his age, as I need the care and consideration of others, I feel I am enabling them to reach a greatness and a potential that they would never have known without reaching out to help me and others like me.

I understand in a wonderful way what our Lord

meant when he said, ". . . unless a grain of wheat falls to the ground and dies, it remains just a seed; but if it dies, it produces much fruit." Until we allow ourselves to be a burden, unless we allow ourselves to be cared for, then new life — new love — cannot grow.

Senior citizens fear that they are no longer useful and productive. I think this denies the existence of a wonderful Creator who is our God. When we are young, we think of what we can do, of all the wonderful accomplishments we can make. When we are older, we are asked to do things that God thinks are best. When our own physical power decreases, we're most able to let God's power work in our lives.

Seniors fear that others will take advantage of them, or that they will lose what they have. What we need to remember is that God told us "to be unattached." He wants us to be unconcerned about the things of here and now. What He says to us is, "to give, to share."

I want to say to all my older friends, "Don't be afraid. Leave the door to your heart open. Don't lock out the world. Sit on your front porch. Let the world see you."

A woman named Lorraine lives down a long, winding dirt road that leads up onto a hill. Her house is not beautiful, but her view of the mountains is magnificent.

Lorraine gets lonely out there, and needs help from time to time, so Jane, one of our volunteers, visits with her and takes her to the grocery store and doctor's appointments and that sort of thing.

Jane is a young woman, and Lorraine is an old woman, and it would seem, on the outside, that Jane does all the giving and Lorraine all the taking. But that's not the way Jane feels about it. She talks of how much Lorraine has taught her about gardening and medicinal plants. She says every time she leaves Lorraine she carries fresh vegetables in her hands, new knowledge in her head, and new wisdom in her heart.

I have seen this time and time again, and it convinces me that of all the people we can assist on this journey, the older people add the most to the pilgrimage. They have faced the forks in the road and survived. They know how to keep their eye on the goal and their heart on the Lord.

They are the best guides we could ever find.

Building Resting Places

Leaving all the memories of Berea behind, I headed south to Rockcastle County and the town of Mt. Vernon, Kentucky, another of my responsibilities in those early days. My first task was to find a place for Sunday services. When I drove past where old "Pop" Reynolds' candy store used to be, I remembered how creative we sometimes had to be.

Pop Reynolds was an elderly gentleman who owned a house with a fairly large living room, which he graciously offered to let us use. We held services there for several months, but it wasn't a good solution. Many people were uncomfortable imposing on the Reynolds family. We always had a handful of tourists, and they were especially reluctant to visit a private home on Sunday.

Next door to Pop's home he had a candy store. The store was divided into two rooms, a front room with the candy counter and ice cream stand, and a back room with a juke box, a potbellied stove, and booths where customers could relax while they ate.

Being quite bold in my youth, I asked Pop if we could use the store for our services.

Pop thought it was a fine idea, so we began to have Sunday services in the candy store. We put a board over the soft drink cooler and that became our altar. The parishioners sat in the booths. It was a pretty strange sight, I'm sure, but we used it as our church for ten years or so.

I'll never forget a little five-year-old boy named Frank who used to pass around our collection plate. He loved the job. I think he must have been the proudest collection-taker in the world. One Sunday, he stopped in front of a couple of tourists. Frank stood in front of the couple with his collection plate and wouldn't move.

Frank's mother whispered, "Frank. Frank. Keep going, Frank."

Frank just stood there.

His mother said, a little louder, "Frank. Keep going. Frank."

Frank ignored her and glared at the couple in front of him. They were beet red by this time.

Finally his mother yelled, "Frank! Move on."

Frank turned to his mother and yelled back, "But they didn't hardly put anything in!"

We eventually got Frank to move on, and the couple left very quickly after the service.

I wish I could have gotten Frank to help me with fundraising to build a church, but we finally found the land and the money to build a church there in

Mt. Vernon. I'll always remember Pop Reynolds' candy store, though.

Building churches was a big part of my early days here in Appalachia. I suppose that was natural. I came from a family of builders. My father was a construction foreman. My grandfather was a carpenter. All of my brothers became carpenters or bricklayers.

As children, my brothers and sisters and I were always building snow houses, castles, and forts in the woods.

So I guess it's no surprise that building was always on my mind. Buildings were important; no pilgrim can walk forever without rest. We all need a place to take a break from the journey from time to time. I always thought of churches as places where we can escape the trials and tribulations of the open road and rest our souls for a little while in the presence of God. A church was also a home for God, a place where we could give thanks.

I wasn't long in Appalachia, however, before I realized another type of building sorely needed to be done. In some ways, it was even more important.

As I visited with poor people in the hollers and valleys of the mountains, I was shocked to see the condition of their houses. Home should also be a place where pilgrims can rest and store up energy for the journey ahead. Yet many of the homes I saw were so uncomfortable and unsafe that they could hardly be places of rest.

Many families lived in what scarcely qualified as

shacks. I met a woman who lived in a chicken coop. I met a family that lived in an old school bus without electricity or water. I met a man who lived in an old, six foot by nine foot camping trailer with a collapsed roof that he tried to repair with an old plastic tarpaulin. I met old people who had to walk a quarter of a mile to haul water. I met families of ten crowded into two small rooms.

I grew up during the Great Depression, and with thirteen mouths to feed, my family struggled to stay one step ahead of the bill collectors, but I had never seen anything like these homes. I was amazed at the strength and perseverance of the people who survived these terrible conditions.

I remember one family with five children. They had been living in a house built on stilts on the side of a hill. The house was in terrible shape and one day it began creaking and groaning and they all ran outside just before it broke off its stilts and slid down the mountain.

They had to have a house, so they cut down the trees on their land to build a log cabin. They patched the gaps in the logs with mud to keep out the wind, but had to stop stacking logs to form walls when they ran out of trees on their land. The ceiling was only five feet high. At six foot-plus, I couldn't stand up inside the house — I could barely get in at all.

I arranged a job for the parents of this family at a greenhouse complex we had started. As they grew in skill and dedication to their new work, we moved them out of that tiny log cabin into a house we had repaired next to the greenhouse.

We eventually sold the greenhouse to the man who managed it for us and I lost touch with the family until just recently. I was at an automobile dealership getting a temporary license plate for an old truck I had bought and as I waited for a salesperson, I admired the newly decorated show room. When I mentioned my admiration of a quality paint job to the salesperson, he said, "Don't you know who painted it? The guy sure knows you. He says you saved his family. You put shoes on their feet, clothes on their backs, and a roof over their heads."

When he told me the young man's name, I cried for joy. It was one of the children from that family with the sad log cabin. I was so happy that he was doing well and had a thriving painting business.

When we saw the incredible need of families like his, we began to help fix their homes and make them more comfortable and safe. Today, our Home Repair Program is one of our most important works.

Using building materials that are donated or purchased and the labor of volunteers and CAP employees, we've helped repair thousands of homes over the years. Sometimes, we provide materials and technical assistance so people can repair their own home and gain the pride that comes from such work.

Sometimes we provide windows to replace plastic. Sometimes we help replace a leaky roof. Sometimes we help repair cracked walls that let the cold mountain wind roar through in winter.

Often we put in pumps and indoor plumbing, especially for older people who are no longer able to use an outhouse or haul water from distant wells. We made many homes safer by replacing or repairing old wood or coal stoves, and fixing ancient, fire-prone wiring.

Sometimes, a home is completely unrepairable. So we have developed low-cost houses we can build from scratch. These small houses aren't mansions, but they are warm and safe and they make an enormous difference to people in need.

This home repair work is incredibly rewarding because it makes such a long-lasting difference in people's lives. It's so much fun that it's one of the favorite things for volunteers to come and do here in the spring and summer.

In 1992 we started hosting "Work Fest" during the college spring break week. This year, 335 students came from 38 different colleges. Instead of going to Florida or some other vacation spot as so many students do, they spent their time fixing houses for the poor in Appalachia.

We recently created a Home Repair Vocational Program to train people in construction and carpentry repair work. There is a shortage of skilled house builders in Appalachia today. This new program fixes the homes of the poor while teaching a trade that can help people earn a living for the rest of their lives.

All over the mountains, we have made people's

lives a little better by helping to create nicer places for weary pilgrims to rest.

To me, this is spiritual work.

For example, a little while back we helped a family after the wiring in their house caught fire. The fire was discovered quickly, so there wasn't much damage to the house, but it was no longer safe. The family didn't have the money or the knowledge to replace the wiring and the power company wouldn't reconnect the house until it was completely rewired.

This crisis was the final straw in a long list of problems, and it sank the family into deep despair. While we were rewiring the house we discovered they had another serious problem. The woman of the house and her 8-month-old baby were both ill from drinking contaminated water from their well. To solve this problem we ran new pipes from a distant water line.

When all this work was done, the couple came to me and poured out their gratitude. Through tears of thanksgiving, the man said, "You know, we had lost hope for the future. It seemed like everything we tried to do failed. We figured we'd never be able to do anything better for our kids. We were like dead people.

"Then you came along, a stranger, and you helped us fix this problem, but even more, you've given us back our hope. How can we ever thank you?"

I told them to pray and help others whenever they could and they assured me they would do both.

A week later, I spoke with them again, and they

told me that until we helped them, they had been considering divorce. The stress of their life was destroying the holy bond between them. The new sense of hope we had given them rekindled their love for each other and we not only saved a house, but also a family — a home.

Restoring hope might be the most important benefit of our Home Repair Program, but another important benefit is teaching people how to do repairs and construction so they can help their neighbors and multiply that hope.

Often, we'll make repairs on the worst house in a neighborhood. Six months or a year later, we find that many of the other houses have been fixed up as well because the people we helped used their new knowledge and hope to help their neighbors.

One of the reasons that building resting places for the weary pilgrims has always meant so much to me is that I have always been saddened by the Christmas story. We usually think of the Christmas story as one of joy, but I often think of how the poor baby and His parents were forced to live in a stable for animals.

I often wonder why God had His only Son born in such a humble place. He certainly could have arranged for Jesus to be born in a palace like the King he was. Instead, He was born in a stable.

God was showing us that He was sending His Son to be a brother to the downtrodden. He wanted us to realize that we all have a responsibility to help those of us who have the least.

Whenever I see a family living in a home that is barely better than a stable, I think of the baby Jesus. If I could do one thing for God, I would go back 2000 years and build a nice home for the Holy Family so our Lord would be warm and safe. I can't do that, but I can do the next best thing by helping to build homes for Him now.

When I started out in Appalachia, I wanted to build churches for Him. I am still doing that. I think beautiful churches are wonderful resting places where pilgrims can rest and restore their souls. But more and more today, I feel we must build homes for Jesus by building them for the least of His brothers and sisters.

Supporting Families on the Journey

On my pilgrimage through Rockcastle County and Mt. Vernon, I drove out U.S. Route 25 and down into Renfro Valley to see a special wall in the playroom at CAP's Family Life Services. On this wall are the brightly colored handprints of dozens of children who have stayed with us.

I love to look at that wall because it symbolizes so much about what we are trying to do at Family Life Services and in all our programs. To see all those hands, of every size, every one unique, yet all alike, and all together in one place, fills my heart with pride.

Family Life Services is part of the Family Life Center, a dream of mine for a very long time. My own family was a source of comfort and inspiration to me when I was a boy. It broke my heart, when I first came to Appalachia, to see how poverty destroyed families in the mountains. I met many couples who loved each other and who loved their children and yet the families were being torn apart by isolation, constant worries about money and jobs, and poor living conditions.

I knew that if we were to create a giant family of pilgrims moving toward a common goal, we had to support individual families. We had to help them cope. We had to give them new opportunities. We had to give them hope.

That is the goal of all our programs. We support families by helping them when emergencies strike. We give them new opportunities by helping parents get their high school equivalency degrees so they can get jobs. We give them hope for the future by helping their kids get a better start in school through our child development centers.

We ease the burden on families by helping them repair their homes. We improve their nutrition through our Garden Seed program. By providing Christmas Baskets filled with food, clothing, toys, and books, we help make sure that even the very neediest family can celebrate Christmas.

We recognize, however, that some families need special help. That's why the Family Life Center and our other special programs for families have become so important.

For example, we try to help families being destroyed by abuse that is often triggered by the stress and despair of poverty and fed by alcohol and drug abuse.

Our spouse abuse centers provide a refuge for women and children, and sometimes men as well. They provide safety while we try to help couples figure out the real problems that are destroying the love between them. Sometimes, the husband and wife reconcile. Sometimes it is impossible.

Not long ago we got a call from a police station where a woman was calling for our help. Marie had left her home with her two children to escape abuse. At CAP's Family Life Abuse Center, she told us her story.

A bright and articulate woman, she could not read or write. Her parents' religion forbade her to attend school. She was married before she was 15 and soon had two children. She was completely isolated and rarely got out of her own yard. One day, an engineer for the electric company was making his rounds, checking equipment and that sort of thing when he knocked on Marie's door to ask a few questions. He was shocked when he saw her purple bruises.

He asked her if she were okay and if he could help her. She said no and he left quietly, but the next day he returned with a card that had the phone number of the Family Life Abuse Center. She didn't tell him she couldn't read the card.

A few days later, Marie fled her home fearing for her life and went to the local police station. When they asked her what she wanted to do, she said, "I want to call these people," and she handed them the card with our number on it.

Marie stayed at the Family Life Abuse Center for several months and then moved to Family Life Services. With a great deal of courage, she decided that she wants to get her high school equivalency degree (GED), even though she has never been to school a day in her life. She is learning to read quickly, however, and I have a feeling she will reach her goal. We also helped her find an apartment where she can be safe with her children.

The happy ending to Marie's story blurs the tragedy underneath, that four people's lives were turned upside down when a family disintegrated. That's why we try so hard to get to families and help them solve their problems before they reach the point of crisis.

At the Family Life Center we offer counseling to couples, parenting classes, education programs, and much more. These are things that you find in most communities across the country nowadays, but they are so important here, where families have so many strikes against them.

Many young people who drop out of school find themselves without a future and fall into despair. Many marry too young, when they are not ready for the responsibility of marriage and children. Many did not have good examples of how to be a parent when they were growing up and now they don't know how to care for their own children.

Appalachia also has many people who practice poor health habits. There are also many people with disabilities. These factors may put stress on families. That's why we created the Community Health Advocates Program, to teach about good mental and physical health, personal hygiene, prenatal care, and parenting skills. And that's why we created the Rainbow Respite and Rejoice Respite care centers, which give the families of adults and children who have disabilities a break from daily responsibilities that can be overwhelming.

As I look back over 45 years and forward to the future, I know we have created good programs to help families. But there is much more we need to do. That's why I have made a promise to God that if He will give me another ten years of pilgrimage on this earth, I will spend it trying to build up families here in Appalachia. I feel this is what He wants me to do.

When God created the earth, He gave us all kinds of beauty in the land, the sky, the oceans, the creatures, and the plants. Then, to top it all, he created the first family — Adam and Eve — and gave them control over the whole universe. He knew that a strong family would protect and reflect the beauty He had created.

Imagine if we had strong families here. Imagine if every family had two loving parents to help each other grow and work together to guide their children and help them dream of a better future. Imagine if the children honored their parents and respected the wisdom of their grandparents. Imagine if families were a place where children learned that violence is never the answer. What if all the members of the family were dedicated to one another and to walking together towards a stronger community. What if each day ended with the family united in prayer, thanking God.

So much good would flow through these mountains — and to the entire country — if every family were like that.

In the previous chapter I talked about how much I love to build things. More than anything else, I want to build families. I want to help repair them and renovate them and make them strong enough to withstand the inevitable storms that come on this journey of life.

When we do that, our steps on this pilgrimage will be lighter and quicker, and we'll reach our goal arm in arm as one big family of love.

Building Bridges for Pilgrims

Garrard County, Kentucky, was one of the four original counties for which I was given responsibility. It eventually became the headquarters of the Christian Appalachian Project and the center of most of our efforts to fight poverty. But when I visited Garrard County and its county seat of Lancaster on my pilgrimage last fall, the memory that came back most strongly was of the chasms that separated people of different faiths when I first came to Appalachia.

I remembered when we were first building a church here. I had gathered the small community of Catholics in the area and we agreed that we wanted to build a church. We contacted Cliff Ledford, the realtor who was later to sell me the land for our first summer camp at Cliffview Lodge. Cliff and I looked at dozens of places without seeing anything that seemed to fit our needs and our dreams for the future. We were about to quit for the day when he said, "Wait a minute. Mr. Calico, the county judge, is building a new house, and I wonder if his old house is for sale. It might fit the bill."

We went to Judge Calico's house and he told us he was building a new house down the street and that his present house was indeed for sale. The house had possibilities, but it was on a very small lot, only about 100 feet deep from the road. That wasn't enough for the dreams we had, so I asked him about the property next to his. On that property was a big old house, one of the first homes built in Lancaster. The owner had died and the heirs were trying to decide what to do with the property. We soon found out that they were interested in selling as well. It also turned out that the property behind Judge Calico's house was for sale. By putting these three properties together, we had what we needed to establish the first Catholic presence in Garrard County.

To some, that was a frightening possibility.

We negotiated a price of about $34,000 for all three properties and I got clearance from Bishop Molloy to purchase them. Cliff Ledford and I went out to do a final walk around the properties and we were about to leave when one of the neighbors called Cliff over to his fence.

The two men talked for several minutes, and I watched Cliff shake his head "no" several times. Then he walked back over to me and we went on our way. Cliff didn't tell me about the conversation until several years later.

He eventually told me the neighbor had said, "Hey, whatever those Catholics are offering, I'll offer

$1,000 more. We don't want any of those people here."

I asked Cliff why he didn't take the neighbor up on that offer. He said, "Because I gave you my word and I don't go back on my word."

I've always been grateful for his integrity. This pilgrimage might have gone down a different road if he hadn't done such a decent thing.

That event, and others in the other three counties, convinced me that there was a great deal of mistrust and fear of Catholics in Appalachia. I couldn't understand that. Most of the people who were objecting to our presence were Christians of other denominations. We had far more in common than we had differences. We all worship the same God. We all believe Jesus is our Lord and Savior. We say the same prayer He gave us, the Lord's Prayer. Why should we hate each other?

I began to see that for my pilgrimage to be successful, I would have to build bridges that connected one community of faith to another. Otherwise, how could we get over the chasms that separated us? How could we join hands and walk toward our common goal to bring God's love to the mountains?

There was so much mistrust. When I tried to build a church in Jackson County, there was strong opposition. One man actually ran me off the road with his pick-up truck. He came at me with fists swinging, threatening to beat me up if I didn't go away forever. When I didn't give in, he had the sheriff arrest me.

They charged me with setting cows and pigs loose and destroying people's property. I was put on trial without a lawyer and fined $120. I had to appeal to the Circuit Court to get the conviction overturned.

Another time, I was preaching on street corners, something I do every summer because I feel strongly that we are all called to spread the good news of the Bible.

After I had finished preaching for the day, a man came up to me with a rifle cradled in his arm. He said, "Are you that Catholic preacher?"

"Yes, I am," I said.

"Well," he said leveling the gun at me, "then I reckon you're the one I'm here to shoot."

I stared down the barrel of his gun and the hair on the back of my neck stood up. It took me a moment to regain my composure.

"Did I say something in my preaching that offended you?" I finally asked.

"No. I didn't hear your preaching. I just heard about you."

"Well, did some other Catholic offend you some time?"

"Buddy," he said, "as far as I know, you're the first one I ever set eyes on."

"If I haven't hurt you and no other Catholics have hurt you, then why do want to shoot me?"

Still holding the gun leveled at me, the man pulled himself up to his full height and looked me in the eye. "Because I'm a patriotic American," he said. I hesitate to repeat the rest of his words of hate, but it's important to understand the depth of this man's fear. "There are three things wrong with America," he said. "The first is the communists. Second, there are the niggers, and then there are the Catholics — and they're worst of all. And if it takes shootin' to keep you people from ruinin' my town, I reckon I will."

I talked him out of shooting me, or I wouldn't be here to write this book today. But it was obvious there was a lot of hidden fear and hatred.

I wanted to heal that hatred and erase that fear. If I couldn't do that, we could never move forward together.

Over the years, I have tried to build bridges between faiths. As we began to help the poor, we never paid any attention to whether the people we helped were Catholics or even Christians. To me, they were all children of God in need.

I have sought out ministers of other denominations and tried to find the common ground. I found that with few exceptions, they were good people who wanted to follow the Lord, and who wanted to help the poor.

And I found that sometimes, courage and kindness can go a long way towards building bridges across even the widest gulf. For example, a few months after that man in Jackson County ran me off the road, I heard his barn had burned down. I sent one of my friends over to him to tell him that some lumber and building materials had been donated to us and we'd like to share it with him.

The man looked at my friend and said, "What's the matter with that preacher? Don't he know how to fight fair?"

I wish I could say we became close friends after that, but that particular chasm was just too wide to cross. He never ran me off the road again, though, so I guess some progress was made.

Over and over again, we extended a hand of friendship to other churches. When they saw that I was not the evil person they had imagined me to be, they extended their hands to me. Those extended hands have built bridges of understanding and trust between the churches of Appalachia.

What a payoff there has been because of those bridges. We've helped hundreds of churches by providing donated furniture and building materials and by helping out wherever we could. They in turn, have helped us, working side by side with us to repair houses, recruit volunteers, and find new ways to help the poor.

Just a few weeks ago, I was visited by a church official from one of the larger Protestant denominations in Kentucky. He said he'd read my books and he wanted to know how our churches could work together to fight poverty. He even asked me if I would speak at their state-wide convention.

I was recently at a meeting of ministers from various faiths and I offered samples of Bible School

materials to the other ministers. Several took copies
to evaluate. Two days later I got a call from one of
the ministers, who wanted to know if he could get
15 sets of the materials. "Of course," I said. When
the man came to my house an hour later, I told him
we had other supplies like soap, napkins, and
children's books about Jesus that might be useful for
Bible School.

When the minister loaded his car, he came to me
and said, "I love you. May I hug you?"

I felt wonderfully honored.

Later that same day I helped load ten oak pews
onto a truck for another church. The minister thanked
me and said, "You help us more than our own people.
Thank you!"

A few days later, I attended a meeting at a local
church. Their minister had just retired and they were
discussing how to find a new minister. One gentleman stood up at the meeting in this Protestant church
and said, "Do you think we could find another Father
Beiting?"

I thank God that He has led me through these 45
years of changes and let me see the beautiful fruit
that has come forth. How far we've come!

In the 45 years of this pilgrimage, I have seen heal-
ing. I have seen bonding. I have seen cooperation in
genuine love between one religious denomination
and another. I am proud to have witnessed this re-
versal.

Sometimes people ask me, "What is your greatest

accomplishment?" I don't waste much time thinking about such things, but I do know that I am very proud to have been a bridge builder, a healer. I have tried to live by Christ's words, "By this shall all know that you are my disciples, that you have love one for another."

I love my own Catholic faith. But with all my heart and soul I know I can't be a good Catholic if I don't love all men and women. If I don't love my fellow Christians and those who have no church or religion as well. I must love them with the same love that Christ has for each and every one of us here.

Here at the Christian Appalachian Project we have bonded a family of nearly 340 employees, 75 permanent volunteers, almost 1,000 temporary volunteers each year, and thousands of faithful supporters all over the country. We're people of all faiths. Our common, overriding desire is to please God and serve one another.

I believe the bridges we have built will continue to serve other pilgrims long after our journey is over. They will continue to span the chasms of mistrust and help pilgrims of the future walk together in peace.

Freeing Captive Pilgrims

After leaving Lancaster, I stopped for lunch at Lane's Restaurant on Route 27 heading north toward Lexington. This little diner was called Buster's Drive-in when I first came to this area. It was a great spot for a restaurant — on top of a hill and convenient for travelers coming south from Lexington on their way to vacation at Herrington Lake.

I was surprised and saddened when it went out of business. I hated to see another local business disappear, so we bought the old restaurant and hired a woman to manage it. She was a wonderful cook and did well for a couple of years. Then she moved away, but by that time the restaurant was thriving and we were able to sell it.

I'm glad we rescued that little diner because it has continued to be a restaurant all these years and has been expanded several times. If it wasn't for our efforts to keep it alive, it might be just another crumbling building by now.

Lane's Restaurant is just one small example of how

we have tried to stop the economic decline of this region and help start an economic revival in the mountains.

After a good lunch at Lane's, I headed to another place where we tried to have an impact in that regard.

About 13 miles north of Lancaster, on the Kentucky River, is a town called Camp Nelson. We used to take trips up there with kids to give them the thrill of boating on the River. One day, the older gentleman who owned the boat dock we used told me he was quitting.

"I have to give up this business," he said. "My health isn't good, this area is dying, and I don't have the energy to try and save it. I wonder if you'd be interested in trying to revive this place."

Well, he shouldn't have made an offer like that to an old history buff like me. I knew that Camp Nelson was loaded with historic sites from the early years of our country. Daniel Boone, a great hero of mine, lived there for one winter when Kentucky was the edge of the Western frontier. Camp Nelson was the site of one of the first two ferries across the Kentucky River. It was a famous crossing place for buffalo. Later, it had the longest covered bridge in America.

Camp Nelson received its name because of the important role it played in the Civil War when it was the headquarters of one of the North's great generals, General Nelson — the only officer in the Civil War to hold a commission from both the Army and the Navy at the same time.

During the war, Camp Nelson was an important destination for escaping slaves; they found safety and a chance to move to freedom farther north.

In the early part of this century, the Army Corps of Engineers began to build locks on the Kentucky River and there was a great deal of commerce up and down the river. Camp Nelson was a big part of that.

The area was loaded with historical significance and interesting tourist attractions. I jumped at the chance to try and revive the area. We built a campground and fixed up the boat docks. We renovated an old restaurant and built a music hall which attracted many famous Kentucky mountain musicians like Old Joe Clark. The distillery across the river gave us a big piece of land they were no longer using. It had a large stone house that was originally built in the late '20s to be a hotel. We had big plans for that.

Walking around, seeing the places where we worked at Camp Nelson, I remember all the research we did to document the historical sites and build tourist interest.

Things were going so well that we were approached by a tourism development company. They wanted to lease and manage our entire operation and we thought that was a great idea. We knew we were not really expert at this business and they were. But we were happy that we had put in enough sweat to get people interested in Camp Nelson again.

Unfortunately, shortly after the management

company took over, we had the biggest flood on the Kentucky River in 100 years and many of the buildings were severely damaged. The management company up and left.

We sold off the various parts of the operation. In one sense, it was a failure. But we did restore interest in Camp Nelson, and just last year the federal government set aside funds to restore and preserve Camp Nelson's many historical sites. I'm sure this area will continue to grow as a tourist attraction and I'm glad we had a part in that.

These are just a couple of examples of how we have tried, over the course of this pilgrimage, to set people free from poverty by providing jobs and business opportunities.

Often in this journey, I have been confronted with needs — food, clothing, medicine, housing — a thousand things. My instinct, like most people, is to answer the immediate need. We have spent a great deal of time and energy trying to meet those needs. There is nothing wrong with this, of course. We have a divine command to feed the hungry and clothe the naked.

But I have learned that charity can't stop there. If it does, then we are simply serving our own needs, our own desire to be wanted and be important. We're not serving the needs of the poor.

In the end, handouts only enslave people and make them dependent. They don't set people free. They don't let people show the world their strengths and talents.

I remember the day, many years ago, when I started a woodworking shop in Jackson County, Kentucky. We specialized in such items as bookends, cutting boards, and candlestick holders. I'll never forget a conversation I had with one of the men we hired.

He spent the first part of the week learning how to operate the equipment. When the week was over, he showed me his work. It was beautiful. He said to me, "I'd be willing to do this kind of thing for nothing. I never knew I could make something like this. I've never been so proud."

His pay meant he could support himself and his family, but in some ways the pride and satisfaction he felt was even more important.

The people of Appalachia have a great deal of ingenuity, perseverance, and determination. I am convinced that if we can give them the opportunities, they can work themselves out of poverty and dependence.

They can set themselves free.

Very early on, we helped one man create a dairy farm. It now has several hundred dairy cows and is completely self-supporting. Another time, we set up a sawmill to take advantage of the hardwood forest resources in eastern Kentucky. It is now the largest one in the area. We helped begin an intensified agriculture greenhouse farm that now brings in sales of a million dollars a year. All these ventures are now operated privately.

We still run a successful Christmas wreath factory that employs 136 people during the weeks leading up to Christmas.

This is only the tip of the iceberg. I have dozens of ideas myself, and the people of Appalachia have many more.

I would love to see a stained glass industry grow here in the mountains. We have a major manufacturing source of glass in West Virginia. Stained glass is in big demand these days for churches, homes, and restaurants. It is a thing of beauty and art that could reflect the nobility of Appalachia and at the same time help set our people free.

A while ago, a friend from the Pittsburgh area donated a silkscreening press and other related equipment. There is a big market these days for clothing with silkscreened logos and other designs and by the time this book is printed, the first shirts and jackets will come off our press.

We also created a ceramics workshop in the basement of an old supermarket. Some of the equipment was donated, some of it we purchased. Now several employees are gaining the satisfaction of good work, and objects of great beauty and value are coming out of that old basement.

I found several highly qualified people to run these businesses and I'm praying they'll be successful. Please pray with me.

We recently helped a local businessman create a company called Appalachian Environmental

Products, which makes a line of outdoor furniture made from recycled plastic milk bottles. The stores that have begun selling the furniture love it and I'm sure it will do well. This new company is not only creating jobs in this area of high unemployment, but it is helping to solve environmental problems as well.

I know that there are a million other ideas. I invite anyone who has business ideas to bring them here. You'll not only have the chance to build a successful business, but by providing jobs, you'll be helping to set the people of Appalachia free.

I also appeal to retiring business people to come here and help us start new businesses in Appalachia. Your skills in financing, management, marketing, and manufacturing could help set people free.

One of the critical needs to creating new businesses is, of course, finding the start-up money. I dream of creating a revolving loan fund that could help meet this need.

I wish that when someone comes to us in need of food or clothing or whatever, we could also point them to a good job that would solve their crisis needs and set them free from the dependency of poverty.

I ask everyone who reads these pages to pray for this new pilgrimage and join me in reviving the economy of Appalachia. Together we can break the chains of poverty and set the people of the mountains free to continue on their pilgrimage towards a brighter future of hope.

Support From Home

When pilgrims of old set off for the Holy Land, they went with the blessings and support of the people back home. The pilgrims' supporters would provide money, food, transportation, and other necessities so they could share in the success and feel the grace that flowed from the pilgrimage.

The same has been true of this pilgrimage of mine and of the Christian Appalachian Project over the decades.

It didn't take long for our work to grow beyond the resources of the local communities. We had to have outside help. We needed sponsors to help us make it to our distant goal.

I began writing to people asking for their help. First it was my personal friends. Then it was Catholics around the country. Eventually, we were writing to all kinds of people who shared in the vision of our pilgrimage.

I have never ceased to be amazed and filled with joy at the generous way people continue to respond. From all corners of America, people have joined this pilgrimage by sending their donations, joining us in prayer, and volunteering their time.

Over the years, thousands have written to tell me how much they felt a part of what we were doing — as if they were walking beside me. Many of them have come to Appalachia to visit us and see how we were helping the poor and trying to defeat poverty in the mountains.

Generous people have helped me in many ways, large and small. In an earlier chapter I mentioned our new Good Samaritan Home. When that idea was just a dream, I talked about it to anyone who would listen. I said I needed land and a building. In looking around, I found a spot that seemed perfect for this new home. I went to the owners of the land and told them of my dream. They told me they didn't have any great plans for that particular piece of land and that they'd swap it with me for another piece of land I owned. It was not at all an even swap — the land they were giving us was worth far more than the land we gave them in return. It was a wonderfully generous thing for them to do.

Then, of course, I had the problem of how to build the house. I didn't have the materials or the labor. Some CAP volunteers said they had a friend in Indianapolis who owned a construction company. They invited him to come and meet with me. When I told him my dream, he said, "As soon as spring comes, I'll bring down eight or nine men and we'll spend a week. It shouldn't take longer than that."

I had the land, I had the labor, all I needed were the materials. I talked to another friend about my dream and how others had donated the land and the labor. She listened quietly but never said anything about helping. A week later, she made a donation large enough to buy all the materials we needed.

In the spring, as soon as the weather was good enough, the donated materials arrived on the donated land, and the volunteer construction crew went to work. A week later there stood the shell of the Good Samaritan Home for homeless families where there had been only bare ground.

To top it off, a friend who lived in Ohio donated thousands of dollars worth of furniture. He had retired and had moved to Florida to a smaller home so he gave us rooms full of fine furniture he no longer needed.

Now that this wonderful place is open for families who have fallen on hard times, we rely on the generosity of people from all over the country who send donations to help operate it.

This is miraculous. Through their generosity, all these people have turned my dream into a reality. Today, when I show people through the Good Samaritan Home, they say to me, "How were you able to build such a nice home in such a nice spot, furnish it with such fine furniture, and keep it going week after week?"

I tell them it's all due to the miracle of generosity. The miracle of generosity has happened so many times in the course of this pilgrimage.

We have seen many donations of materials, beginning when I asked people to donate clothing, food, and household goods for our Attic Stores. Over the years, the donations have become more varied, more valuable, and even more effective at providing comfort and hope to people in poverty.

A few examples come to mind. There was the friend, who has since passed away, who owned a sash and door company. From time to time, he would send his workers through his warehouse to gather up all the merchandise that was no longer carried in the catalogs. We'd get truckloads of doors and windows we could use in our building and home repair projects.

There is a furniture company that regularly sends us scratched or nicked furniture by the truckload. Many people have donated used automobiles to provide transportation for our volunteers and employees as they visit isolated families and senior citizens in the mountains. Others have donated mobile homes we can use to provide better housing for families in need.

A few years ago, we created what we call Operation Sharing to help coordinate and distribute the donated goods and materials that come to us from all over the country. In 1994, we received nearly $17 million worth of such materials.

We store these materials in warehouses and then send them where they are most needed in communities all over Appalachia.

Last year we delivered a truckload of goods to a struggling town in West Virginia. We sent 25 rolls of roofing material, 60 rolls of insulation, 400 gallons of paint, 24 bales of clothing, 700 boxes of rice, and many other useful things.

Operation Sharing brings books to people studying for their high school equivalency diplomas. It brings soap and toothbrushes to children learning about hygiene. It brings food to food pantries and soup kitchens.

We even received a truckload of stuffed animals from an amusement park that could be used to provide gifts to children who have few toys.

I think this is a wonderful way for the business world to show its concern for the poor.

In many ways, America has supported this pilgrimage with great generosity.

So many times we've been helped by the generosity of our friends. Sometimes it comes in the form of large donations like those that helped create the Good Samaritan Home. More often, it comes in the form of thousands and thousands of smaller gifts from people all over the country. That steady support is the lifeline that keeps this pilgrimage going and keeps turning dreams into reality, and my prayers go out to all the friends who sacrifice to support our work.

It is only right that I should pray for those who have helped us, because their prayers are another source of strength and generosity. I firmly believe that prayer is the most powerful force in the world. God promised that He would always hear our prayers and give us what we need. You can't get a better promise than that.

In fact, I believe that the best way I can say thanks to all those who've helped us is to pray for them and offer up for them the pains of my pilgrimage.

Often, when the day has run its course, and this weary pilgrim has to rest, I find myself on my back porch with my prayer book. When I am finished reading, I say to the Lord, "How can I ever thank those who have helped so much? What can I possibly do that would repay their generosity?"

The answer I've received is, "Give them to me. I can repay them as no one else can. I know their needs better than they do themselves. I know their hopes and dreams. I know the exact time when help will be most needed and appreciated."

One of my privileges as a Catholic priest is that each day I find myself at the altar of God. When I am there I often say a prayer of thanks for the people who have helped me over the 45 years of this pilgrimage. "Lord," I say, "Will you bless them? Give them peace? Give them happiness?"

I know He hears that prayer because so many of our supporters tell me how much joy and satisfaction they get from joining this pilgrimage with their generosity.

While I am in church I also pray that those friends will continue to help whenever they can. I pray that they will continue to sacrifice to provide us the support that is the backbone of the Christian Appalachian Project. I pray that companies will continue to find ways to send us goods and materials we can use. I pray that all our friends will continue to generously offer their prayers and their sufferings for us and the poor of Appalachia.

I pray that they all will continue to support this wonderful pilgrimage.

The Immortal Pilgrim

It is early morning as I commit to paper my final thoughts about 45 years of pilgrimage. Night has not yet been driven away and the bright sunlight has not yet appeared. In a way this is symbolic of my pilgrimage.

The past 45 years are fading, and yet the dawning of my future journey has not yet begun.

I stand waiting for that dawn, eager to resume the journey. I am well aware of my frailties. My youth has long since disappeared. Even middle age is now solidly behind me. I look back on the past with pride and a deep sense of accomplishment, but I know that much of the task still remains.

The problems have not been solved. There are still too many people trapped in poverty and despair in these beautiful mountains.

The hurts have not all been taken away. There are still too many people suffering. There is still too little hope.

I look up to the heavens this morning, watching for the first light of dawn, and say, "Lord, I wish I didn't have to go. I wish I could stay until the battle has been won — until this pilgrimage is complete."

I guess I want to be immortal.

I know my soul is immortal and I hope that someday I will spend eternity with my Father in heaven. But I want to be immortal here on earth.

I also know that my body cannot possibly survive too much longer. Everyone returns to the dust from which they came.

But still, I want there to be a way that my dreams, my struggles — my pilgrimage — could go on after my Lord has called me home.

I believe the Christian Appalachian Project is one of the ways for that to happen. It is a chance for me, and all the people who join with me, to be immortal here on earth.

It is a way for our love for God and our love for our brothers and sisters to live on forever.

I think back to those early days when we decided to incorporate Cliffview Lodge, our first summer camp for children of poverty. I wanted that camp to be an independent organization so that it would live on, with or without me.

As we added programs to help the poor in other ways, I wanted to make sure they, too, would continue no matter what happened to me.

In 1962 this concern became strong enough in me that I decided to create an organization that could contain all the various efforts we had created and protect them from the vagaries of fate. I decided to call it the Christian Appalachian Project (CAP).

I liked that name because I wanted it clear that Christ was first in everything we did. I like the word "project" because I wanted CAP to be an organization that performed work as opposed to talking about problems. I wanted CAP to be an institution with dirt under its fingernails.

When I was in Lancaster on my pilgrimage, I went to see some of CAP's original homes. CAP first existed in extra space in the church rectory and school. It didn't take long before it was impossible to contain such a rapidly growing organization there.

I thought about buying another house near the church. There was a house a few blocks away that was up for auction. I went to the auction and did my best, but the price just went too high. The auctioneer was my friend Cliff Ledford, the realtor who sold me that first property for a church in Lancaster and who later sold me the property that became Cliffview Lodge.

Cliff came up to me after the auction and said, "Father, it's too bad you didn't win this time. But what about that big house across the street from the church. That just came up for sale."

The house was perfect. It was big and had enough land for parking. We were able to get a good deal on it and we used the bottom floor for offices. We housed volunteers upstairs.

The paint on that old house was peeling terribly so we scraped it and painted the house with hundreds of tiny cans of donated yellow paint. For a long time it was called "The Yellow House," and many important decisions and plans were made there.

Because of those decisions and plans, it wasn't long before we outgrew the Yellow House. We bought another house nearby for the volunteers. Soon, even that wasn't enough.

At that time there was a company in Lancaster called the Cowden Manufacturing Company, which made overalls and denim jeans and other clothing. They had a big manufacturing plant and a large warehouse in Lancaster. They decided to move their warehousing facility to Lexington, leaving the Lancaster warehouse empty.

When I found out the warehouse was for sale, I knew it would be a perfect home for CAP. The Cowdens were asking $225,000. They came down to $175,000 pretty quickly, but that wasn't good enough.

I went and talked to Mr. Cowden and his son at their office in Lexington.

"Look," I said, "I have $125,000. And that's all there is. It's important that you sell this building to CAP."

Mr. Cowden and his son went out of the room for a few moments.

When they returned they said, "We'll take it."

That empty warehouse on Crab Orchard Road in Lancaster has been the headquarters of the Christian Appalachian Project ever since.

Some years later, I saw Mr. Cowden at a function in Lexington.

He said, "Father, it's good to see you again. Come over here, I want you to meet my wife."

When he introduced us, his wife said, "Why, he's the man who bought that building from you in Lancaster."

Mr. Cowden looked at me with a smile and turned back to his wife. "No, dear," he said, "He's that man who *stole* that building from me in Lancaster."

As I sit here on my back porch, I remember that story and I chuckle to myself. "So many odd steps it has taken to get here," I say to the gurgling of the Big Sandy River.

The first light of the sky warns me that dawn is coming and soon it will be time to get going on the day.

I feel that way about my pilgrimage.

So many steps. So many yet to go.

Will I be able to make them all? Will I be around to see the end of this journey? Will I be here when poverty is finally sent running from God's beautiful mountains and His people are finally set free?

The dawn of a new stage in this pilgrimage is coming. Will I be here to take the first step?

I hope and pray so.

Will I be here to take the last steps?

No.

This pilgrimage — this dream — is too big to be contained in one lifetime. I have to find a way to keep the dream alive when I am gone.

It seems to me there are two ways to do that. Two ways that have to work together.

The first is that I have to spend the coming years telling as many people as possible about this dream. I have to set their hearts on fire about this pilgrimage.

No dream dies as long as people hold it in their hearts.

The second is that I have to make sure the Christian Appalachian Project continues into the future to serve as a vehicle to turn those dreams into reality.

Writing this book is part of my effort to meet my first objective. I hope it will inspire many pilgrims to join with me and help me hold this dream high as we walk together. I hope everyone who supports the Christian Appalachian Project will continue to do so in the future.

The second objective is something I am working on and praying about constantly.

I dream of creating an endowment fund to ensure the future of CAP. If we could create a big enough endowment fund, it could be invested so that we could pay for CAP's programs with the interest and never touch the principal.

In this way, our contributions, our love, would go on forever.

Yesterday I went to visit two children in a foster home. These twin boys, five years old, had been taken from their parents because of severe neglect.

Neither of them has even learned to speak.

With an endowment fund, we could help these boys for many years to come. We'll touch the lives of these children until they are old enough to take care of themselves, until they are healed, until they are able to stand on their own two feet.

We'll touch all the others who come after them as well. Though we will disappear from the face of this earth, our spirits will not. Our dreams will not. Our power will not. Our love will not.

We must create this fund. We must always keep putting one foot in front of the other with our eyes on the goal.

We must keep our hand in God's and look to His guidance when the road is dark. We must hold each other's hands and sing out loud when the sun is shining. We must help weary travelers we meet on the road and welcome them into our family of pilgrims.

Most of all, we must keep looking for Jesus' footprints on the ground and follow them as He visits with His people in the mountains.

I know we can do all this. I know the best is yet to be. Come join me in this never ending pilgrimage to ennoble the Holy Land of Appalachia and its people.

I want to end this book with the words to a song written by Daniel Schutte called "City of God" that beautifully expresses my dream:

City of God

Awake from your slumber!
Arise from your sleep!
A new day is dawning
For all those who weep.

The people in darkness
Have seen a great light.
The Lord of our longing
Has conquered the night.

Let us build the city of God.
May our tears be turned into dancing!
For the Lord, our Light and our Love,
Has turned the night into day!

We are sons of the morning;
We are daughters of day.
The One who has loved us
Has brightened our way.

The Lord of all kindness
Has called us to be
A light for his people
To set their hearts free.

Let us build the city of God.
May our tears be turned into dancing!
For the Lord, our Light and our Love,
Has turned the night into day!

CITY OF GOD, © 1981, Daniel L. Schutte and New Dawn Music, P.O. Box 13248, Portland, OR 97213. All rights reserved. Used with permission.

THE MOUNTAIN SPIRIT

Our bimonthly magazine, *The Mountain Spirit*, will keep you up-to-date on the work of the Christian Appalachian Project as we continue to help the people of this poverty-stricken area help themselves. In the magazine, you will also find moving, inspiring stories about the people we serve. If you would like to subscribe to this publication (or renew your subscription), please complete the order form below.

THE MOUNTAIN SPIRIT Subscription Order Form

Please enter my one-year subscription to *The Mountain Spirit*. I have enclosed my check for $6.00, made payable to CAP.

Name _____

Address _____

City _____ State _____ Zip _____

Please return this Order Form, along with your check, to: Christian Appalachian Project, 322 Crab Orchard Road, Lancaster, KY 40446-0001.

Volunteering With
THE CHRISTIAN APPALACHIAN PROJECT:

☐ I am interested in volunteering for one year. Please send information.

Name _____

Address _____

City _____ State _____ Zip _____

Please return this form to: Christian Appalachian Project, 322 Crab Orchard Road, Lancaster, KY 40446-0001, (606) 792-2219.

If You'd Like to
Know More About the
Christian Appalachian Project . . .

For more information about CAP, or for additional
copies of *Pilgrimage of a Country Preacher*,
please write or phone us at our headquarters:

Christian Appalachian Project
322 Crab Orchard Road
Lancaster, KY 40446-0001
(606) 792-3051

Thank you for your interest and support!